EXIT WITHOUT THE EXIT

I0049101

EXIT

WITHOUT THE

EXIT

Build an eight-figure business that
continues to grow without you

TOM GARDNER

INTERNATIONAL BESTSELLING AUTHOR

GRAMMAR
FACTORY
— EST? 2013 —

Exit Without the Exit
Copyright © 2024 by Tom Gardner.
All rights reserved.

Published by Grammar Factory Publishing, an imprint of MacMillan
Company Limited.

No part of this book may be used or reproduced in any manner
whatsoever without the prior written permission of the author,
except as permitted under copyright law and in the case of brief
passages quoted in a book review or article. All enquiries should be
made to the author.

Grammar Factory Publishing
MacMillan Company Limited
25 Telegram Mews, 39th Floor, Suite 3906
Toronto, Ontario, Canada
M5V 3Z1

www.grammarfactory.com

Gardner, Tom.
Exit Without the Exit: Build an Eight-Figure Business That
Continues to Grow Without You / Tom Gardner.

Paperback ISBN 978-1-998528-09-7
eBook ISBN 978-1-998-528-10-3

1. BUS071000 BUSINESS & ECONOMICS / Leadership.
2. BUS041000 BUSINESS & ECONOMICS / Management.
3. BUS012000 BUSINESS & ECONOMICS / Careers / General.

Production Credits
Cover design by Designerbility
Interior layout design by Setareh Ashrafologhalai
Book production and editorial services by Grammar Factory
Publishing

Grammar Factory's Carbon Neutral Publishing Commitment
Grammar Factory Publishing is proud to be neutralizing the carbon
footprint of all printed copies of its authors' books printed by or
ordered directly through Grammar Factory or its affiliated companies through the purchase of Gold Standard-Certified International
Offsets.

Disclaimer
The material in this publication is of the nature of general comment
only and does not represent professional advice. It is not intended
to provide specific guidance for particular circumstances, and it
should not be relied on as the basis for any decision to take action
or not take action on any matter which it covers. Readers should
obtain professional advice where appropriate, before making any
such decision. To the maximum extent permitted by law, the author
and publisher disclaim all responsibility and liability to any person,
arising directly or indirectly from any person taking or not taking
action based on the information in this publication.

"Founders find true freedom when their business becomes a well-oiled machine, thriving on its own."

UNKNOWN

For Richard. Blue skies.

CONTENTS

INTRODUCTION: KICKING YOU OUT OF YOUR BUSINESS

W hat kind of Founder are you? Are you free and enjoying the fruits of your success? Or has your success trapped you? At the top of every industry, there are celebrated Founders. Founders that have built amazing, high-impact businesses. Founders that have gone on to build second, third, and fourth businesses, or have invested in meaningful, philanthropic ventures. There are also those successful Founders that are simply enjoying the fun, freedom, and flexibility that their businesses have given them. Working *on* their businesses instead of in them. Working on their families, and their relationships. Working on their golf handicap, or whatever they like.

Sadly, some Founders don't get to truly enjoy the fruits of their decades' worth of labor. Some Founders end up trapped by their own success. Founders who are still the glue for their businesses, trapped by lack of structure and "corporate" know-how. Founders who are still the rainmaker and the backbone of sales. Founders who are trapped by capital, shareholders, and the associated aggressive performance expectations.

Does this sound like you?

It's truly heartbreaking to see these Founders becoming anxious, neurotic, and unhappy. The more successful their businesses become, the less they get to celebrate, because it means more pressure on their shoulders. They're like a hamster on a wheel, running non-stop, until they're finally "freed" by a heart attack or some other life-altering (or even life-ending) experience.

But it doesn't have to be that way. You can free yourself from your business *without* compromising its success. In fact, by learning how to "exit without the exit," so to speak, your business is far more likely to thrive.

I know this because I've seen it firsthand—many, many times. My Founder-freeing journey began over fifteen years ago...

MY QUEST TO FREE FOUNDERS

I'll never forget standing in front of a chaotically scribbled-on whiteboard, stepping back and looking at the Founder, and saying, utterly defeated, *"It's not going to work."*

We had spent three hours scribbling, erasing, and revising the thinking on the board, over and over, until we had finally run out of space. It was then that we realized we needed to make some big changes.

We were in a life insurance business. Just months earlier, we had set an audacious three-year target (multiplying our client base by ten times) and a one-year mission: "Free the Founders."

I had been brought in because the Board was getting impatient. The Founders had decided to raise capital, and things just weren't growing fast enough. To add insult to injury, the real value-kicker was getting the

Founders *out* of the business. The broader strategy was to relocate them internationally to do what they did best: start a business, not run one.

The problem was that the Founders were *stuck* running the business, and they were holding it back. This stunted growth annoyed the Board, and perpetuated the **Founder Trap**.

My job was to re-engineer operations and kick the Founders out of the business.

I aligned the Board around our dual business and Founder strategies, making sure they were realistic. We refined the strategy and aligned on a mission. We had a vision launch, and plastered the office walls with taglines and iconography. We had mugs made for the 200 salespeople I had hired (remember, they had capital that they weren't spending).

Everyone was fired up and on board.

Fast forward a couple of months, and it just wasn't working. The 200 new salespeople were struggling. They needed a simpler process. A better system. Something less complicated, more scalable. Simply throwing more people and good managers at the problem wasn't going to be enough.

I had spent the morning with one of the new members of the management team, unpacking what it would take to systematize the process they were running. The key question was:

"What would we need to do to make the business non-Founder-led and scalable?"

The answer was a lot more complicated than I had bargained for going into the problem-solving session. I got on a flight back to head office, pulled the Founder CEO into the boardroom, and unpacked the news.

THAT DAY, AND THAT CONVERSATION, CATALYZED A CHAIN OF EVENTS THAT WOULD REVOLUTIONIZE THE COMPANY.

Six months after that fateful day, we had redesigned the product, pricing, processes, and systems. We increased monthly sales volumes by a factor of **five times, using only 20% of the salespeople.**[1] In just six months! They were swamped with new business!

Had the Board and Founders not explicitly taken action to "Free the Founders," I don't think we would have pushed ourselves to unlock the latent value in the business.

While the business wasn't insignificant by any means, it was still small. As mentioned, the Founders made the calls. Any decisions went via the CEO. The Founders didn't hire decision makers. Decision makers are often perceived as "dangerous" because they have opinions, take initiative, and, of course, try to make decisions.

With smallness, you can have centralized decision making. You don't need management systems when you're small. Everyone is right there, listening to what the Founders tell them. It feels agile. It feels dynamic. It feels safe.

But it *stays* small. Or it doesn't grow fast enough. In this case, the opportunities were huge, but the Founders were stuck doing operational work, not spending enough time on things that would add growth and value. With the Founders spread so thinly, there weren't enough eyes on the various pieces of the business—uncovering opportunities, solving problems, and adding leverage.

Deep down, it wasn't ignorance that was the problem. These were really smart people who had worked in tier 1 consulting and investment banking.

IT WAS EMOTIONAL. THE BUSINESS WAS THEIR BABY.

The team was their family. This was their legacy. Their retirement fund. They had poured heart, soul, sweat, and mortgages into the business. The micromanagement, the fear of letting go, the lack of trust in others— these were all natural, and understandable, behaviors. This business

---

[1] The other 80% were redeployed downstream to customer service-related departments.

was their baby, and they didn't want to give it to someone else in case that person dropped it.

So, I worked with them and fixed that.

The year after re-engineering the business, it moved into a new 5,000-square-meter[2] office space to cater for the growth it was experiencing. Three months later, **the building burned down**.

The business operating system took this in its stride. The business went into disaster recovery mode, and *only lost one sales day*. A week later, the Founder CEO and I were having coffee. He looked up at me and said, *"Well, I guess that's disaster recovery done. What should we do next?"*

So, we kept moving and launched a whole new product and sales team in disaster recovery. All the while still looking for and setting up another new 5,000-square-meter home!

The business won an award for Best Global Disaster Recovery. A year after that, it won the Unilever Prince of Wales Award for Business in the Community. The Founders all left the business, moved abroad with their families, and started their international business.

WATCH IT GROW WITHOUT LETTING IT GO

Time and time again, I've seen Founders (and business leaders in general) fall into the growth-limiting trap of having relatively poor management structures *and* poor management systems.

AMAZING MANAGERS WHO DON'T NEED MANAGEMENT SYSTEMS (IN OTHER WORDS, FOUNDERS) CAN ONLY GET THE BUSINESS SO FAR. GROWTH AND SUSTAINABILITY RELY ON AVERAGE MANAGERS WITH A GREAT BUSINESS OPERATING SYSTEM.

I've worked with countless Founders—as a colleague, advisor, and consultant—and I've come to recognize the symptoms well:

---

[2]   5,000 square meters = ~53,000 square feet.

"There is so much opportunity here. Why can't we move faster?"

"I'll be on holiday next week. But don't worry—I'll be on Zoom every morning."

"Why do I have to do everything?"

And, behind closed doors, *"This will all fall apart without me. Maybe I'm just a bad leader..."*

Let's be honest. Joining the dots of a high-growth business and getting (the right) shit done is hard.

Trying to figure out where to play, how to play, and where to go is hard.

Trying to align managers, and staff, is hard.

Trying to change the way things are done, to work differently and move differently, is hard.

Trying to get and maintain clarity, on how you are doing and what is in the way, is hard.

Trying to get people to do their best day in and day out, with a myriad of personal motivations, challenges, and moods, is hard.

But the hardest task of all is trying to do all of this in your own head, as an emotionally attached Founder. Now *that's* hard.

What's hard for me is watching the struggle. Watching Founders grow great businesses and a tight-knit team, then seeing them lose their spark—get tired and jaded, frustrated with the opportunities they can see but that always seem out of reach. All the while becoming more anxious about being trapped, and the business being over-reliant on them.

IT'S HARD WATCHING FOUNDERS VACILLATE BETWEEN THE RATIONAL, KNOWING THAT SOMETHING NEEDS TO CHANGE, AND THE EMOTIONAL DEFENSE OF INSISTING THAT IT COULDN'T POSSIBLY WORK ANY OTHER WAY.

Well, there is a way.

As the former COO of three high-growth and successful startups, I've said this time and time again to my (naturally anxious) management teams when I have left these roles:

> **"MILLIONS OF OTHER SUCCESSFUL BUSINESSES IN THE WORLD RUN PERFECTLY WELL WITHOUT ME."**

And I've proven that. As COO of these companies, I've grown great management teams with great structures, and transitioned out of the businesses when they outgrew me.

And now I do it for others.

As a Founder, freeing yourself from your business is surprisingly simple once you have the business operating system to do it. The key is to adopt a methodical approach to implementing, assessing, and correcting the business operating system so that it's self-sustaining.

> **THE SHIFT™ BUSINESS OPERATING SYSTEM IS THAT METHODICAL APPROACH.**

Without commitment, you can't tackle the big problems holding you, as a Founder, and your business back. Without a system—specifically, the SHIFT™ Business Operating System—there isn't the time, capacity, or know-how to re-engineer the key parts of the business to make it fly free and high.

> **WITHOUT COMMITMENT AND A SOLID BUSINESS OPERATING SYSTEM, FOUNDERS CAN EASILY FALL INTO THE TRAP OF "WELL, WE TRIED OUR BEST. RUNNING AND GROWING A BUSINESS IS JUST HARD. GUESS I'M HERE TO STAY..."**

We read about the success stories and the business-school case studies—the compelling visions, the innovative strategies, the groundbreaking products. But we get little insight into the business operating system that allowed Founders to take their inspiration and ideas and build self-sustaining and scalable businesses.

By the end of *Exit without the Exit*, you will understand what this business operating system is, and how it can free you. You'll understand how to establish the core spheres of this ecosystem and make them stand alone. Your team will know how to "move the strategic needle" for your business—how to measure progress and course correct, without you.

If you follow the plan in this book and do the work to develop your business operating system, you'll be able to rapidly build an eight-figure business that *grows without you.*

Best of all, you'll be free to watch your legacy grow without letting it go—unlocking more growth potential for your business, and freedom and flexibility for you.

So, let's get to it. Let's kick you out of your business!

CHAPTER 1
THE FOUNDER TRAP

B efore exploring the trap you may find yourself in as a Founder, and some of the ways this might manifest itself in your business, we will take a quick look at four key phases of business growth. This sets you up to contextualize the difference between *business builders* and *business runners*. As a business builder, these insights will help you understand how, and typically where, the Founder Trap emerges in the first place.

KEY PHASES OF BUSINESS GROWTH

Regardless of size and scale, businesses do grow up. Based on my experience, I believe there are four key phases of business growth: startup, growth, running, and corporate.

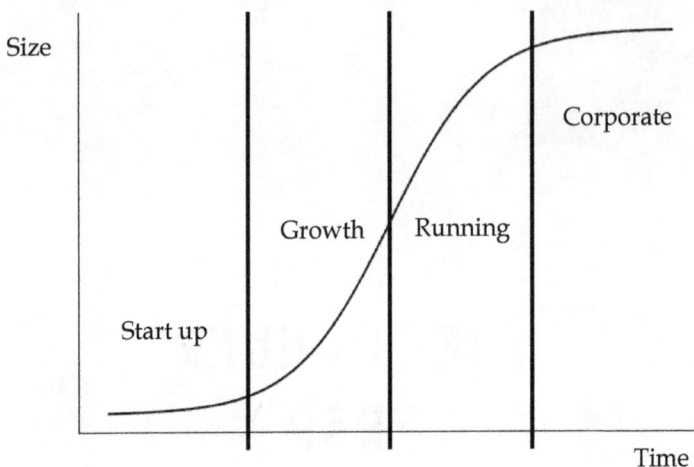

Startup

All businesses were startups once—even Coca-Cola. Whether you knowingly or unknowingly set out to start a "company," this is a time of dynamism, energy, anxiety, and "hustle" for you as the Founder.

From a staff-complement perspective, I would say this stage lasts until you have around ten, maybe twelve staff members. You can all sit around a dinner table; everything is "fluid" and "one team." Being the Founder of the business, you are everything. You take on all senior roles, and, unless you have a business partner, the first ten staff are seldom senior hires. You hire staff to take up the slack, do the admin, follow behind you, and mop up.

Growth

In this phase of business growth, you generally have between ten and fifty staff. (Of course, this depends on business type. In a high-volume, call center–type business, for example, I would exclude frontline staff from the total number.)

This is when you, the Founder, have to start letting go and allow things to happen without your involvement. This is when "meetings" and "reporting" might start happening.

Running

In successful "running" businesses, the company has achieved sufficient scale and system that it can continue to operate and grow *with different managing directors, with different senior managers, through different economic times.*

For some businesses, this is when they start moving from fifty to 500 staff. This is when stakeholder management and management systems become important. There are too many decision makers to get into a room and bash something out. Without the right systems and structures, the business simply doesn't get this far. It may grow and then shrink back to a "Founder-manageable" size.

For others, it's about time. For some businesses, extreme growth and size is just not the plan. As a Founder, you may be happy with a $20 million business and don't want the complexity (or have the hunger) of trying to turn the business into a behemoth.

So, what changes? Time does. The business settles down. It finds its groove. And it finds its groove around you as the Founder and the team. However, once you get to a point where the business feels established and "safe," it starts getting boring! **You have a bunch of business builders trying to run a business!** And they are invariably not passionate or good at *running* a business—they are good at *starting* a business! (More on builders-versus-runners in a moment.)

Corporate

The last phase of business growth is corporate, typically characterized by 2,000-plus staff. There are divisions, politics, business units, "head office" and so forth. This is a whole different level of pain.

Builders versus runners

We are concerned with the "between" phases: growth and running.

As you will have noticed, I haven't categorized phases of growth by revenue, or customers, or annual recurring revenue (ARR), or any other metric. Rather, I have based the growth phases on people. The number of people drastically changes the complexity of the business.

So what?

THERE ARE BUILDERS AND THERE ARE RUNNERS. AND WHEN BUILDERS GET STUCK IN A RUNNER'S JOB, IT'S NOT USEFUL OR SUSTAINABLE.

I am a builder, not a runner. I work well in a business in the startup and growth phases. Once my startups have moved to the 200-plus people mark, over a three- to five-year period, I have built the systems and processes to be able to hand over operations to a runner. This process frees me up to be a builder once more. While I do like starting businesses, I love growing a business and then handing it over to a runner.

I am a builder of business structure and systems. Figuring this out early on in my career has saved me from **"the trap."**

ARE YOU TRAPPED IN YOUR BUSINESS?

So, what is the trap? The trap that you as a Founder could very well get caught in, holding you and your business back?

Firstly, "the trap" is somewhat inevitable.

Most businesses start by bootstrapping. A Founder has an idea. And the first step in making that idea a reality is for that Founder to turn into salesperson, product developer, marketing manager, delivery driver, dishwasher, and CEO.

I absolutely *love* talking to Founders about these wild and scary "startup" days. It's fun. It's hard. It's exciting. You learn *so* much about your customers, your product, your business, and yourself—*so* quickly.

And it feels like yesterday.

Because, before you know it, you are surrounded by a team of twenty, fifty, 500 people, and it's like, "Shit, how did that happen?" With all your intellectual property, your rainmaker history, your commitment and drive, and your ownership of the business, **one day you realize you're essentially trapped by the thing you created**.

From my time in the Founder trenches, here are some reflections on common pitfalls that trap Founders.

You are the strategy document

Many Founder-led companies don't have a strategy. They may not even have a budget. The Founder and senior managers may hold some level of groupthink of what is important over the next three months, but that's it. Bigger decisions are left up to them, and everyone else simply does what they're told.

This is slow, limiting, and inefficient. It can be stressful, unfulfilling, and purposeless for the other leaders and/or managers of these businesses—let alone the staff.

In many other businesses, strategy is viewed as a high-level boardroom concept. It's treated almost like a static document, opened and closed once a year for the Board, just before budget reviews. Rarely is it a living, breathing toolkit. This disconnect can be detrimental (as the following example highlights), as the true power of strategy lies in its ability to drive every decision and action you take.

When a frontline team member sees a strategy with vague phrases like, "Take advantage of opportunities," or "Grow as fast as possible," or "Be the best XYZ company out there," they'll be left wondering, "What the hell does that mean?" That's a good indicator that the business leaders really haven't done their jobs.

In a Founder-led business, the Founder is the walking, breathing strategy document. Remove the Founder and you need to replace that "role" with an actual embedded strategy.

The opportunity is transforming strategy from a theoretical exercise into a practical, everyday toolkit. A strategy should not be something "in the mind of the boss." It should be an active part of discussions, decisions, and the daily grind. It should inform priorities, direct resources, and inspire innovation. Strategy aligns and guides the team, *daily*.

> **STRATEGY PROVIDES A CLEAR (ALBEIT WINDING) PATH THAT EVERYONE UNDERSTANDS AND FOLLOWS.**

To make this a reality, *you need to deliberately build a strategy*. Then you cascade it, ensuring that it's articulated, clear, and *relevant* to everyone in the business. You must distill it and simplify it, so that its goals are clear and actionable. And most importantly, you must live it. You need to embed strategic thinking into your management and performance culture, so that every employee can see how their contributions move the needle, identify what is standing in the way, and do something about it—without you, the Founder.

Your head is in the clouds

It can often seem like it (as much as it might hurt to admit it). Part of the problem with being "the boss" is that you can't be everywhere at once, so you end up having a broad but shallow idea of what is really going on. As a result, a lot of your strategic thinking is "in the clouds," and doesn't connect well with what is happening on the ground. The bigger the business, the bigger the problem.

This is frustrating for you as the Founder, and equally as frustrating—if not more so—for your staff!

Once you have a clear and deliberate strategy, you need to figure out how you tactically deliver it. While the business strategy lays out the "what" and the "why," it can overshadow the operating strategy, which covers the "how" and the "who." The result?

TEAMS FLOUNDER WITH DIRECTIONS THAT SEEM CLEAR TO THE FOUNDER, BUT ARE FAR REMOVED FROM REAL-LIFE, ON-THE-GROUND OPERATIONS.

To bring strategy down to earth, you need to re-envision strategy not just as a destination, but also as a roadmap that includes clear milestones, available resources, and real-world challenges. It requires you to be honest about your current capabilities, what you need to develop, and the tangible steps required to get from point A to point B to point C.

Effective strategy execution requires an operating model that marries vision with practice. It involves aiming high while also digging deep, to ensure you have the skills, resources, and operating systems to turn strategic visions into reality—and without you as the Founder needing to play the instruments on behalf of the musicians in the orchestra.

YOU NEED TO PUT YOUR STRATEGY TO WORK. YOU DO THIS WITH A DELIBERATE AND ALIGNED OPERATING MODEL.

Your business lacks strategy cascading

Many Founders simply communicate their strategy, because the size of their business means they haven't needed to do the real work of cascading it. In smaller businesses, you don't need to, as everyone is "in the same room."

This further exacerbates the disconnect between where you want to get to and operational realities. Communicating a strategy involves more than just sharing information in a captivating and effective way.

CASCADING STRATEGY MEANS EMBEDDING THE STRATEGY INTO EVERY LEVEL OF OPERATION. IT MEANS TURNING STRATEGY INTO ACTIONABLE OBJECTIVES, PROJECTS, AND TASKS THAT EVERYONE CAN WORK ON—WITHOUT YOU, THE FOUNDER, TELLING THEM TO.

Too often, and particularly when a business is small, strategy is treated as a series of announcements at work-related gatherings, or through company-wide emails. Without the necessary follow-through—**where teams interpret, adapt, and implement these strategies in their daily tasks**—it remains just that: a series of announcements. True strategy cascading requires integration with how managers work, make decisions, and focus their teams on the right performance metrics.

STRATEGY NEEDS TO BE LIVED AND BREATHED ACROSS THE ORGANIZATION, NOT JUST PACKAGED IN CAPTIVATING, OFF-THE-CUFF NARRATIVES BY THE FOUNDER.

You have a disconnect between strategy and structures

One of the most persistent challenges I see in businesses of all sizes is the disconnect between strategy and the organizational structures (departments, roles and responsibilities, and capabilities) of the business. A company meticulously crafts a great strategy, then stifles it by following rigid, outdated structures and ways of working.

The main issue is that established organizational structures drive ways of working that can resist change and obscure a clear picture of what is really going on. The way your business is organized and "who does what" can offer subconscious safety and stability, especially during times of significant growth and change. The problem is that some organizational structures drive a particular way of working and looking at the business, which can become strategic obstacles if misaligned. Then it is left to the Founder to step in and try to solve the problem.

I worked with a successful tech company that was a couple of decades old. We started with a strategic review of the business and the market potential. The Founder could very clearly tell me what the business did—what products they sold and to whom. He could not tell me how they did it or how well they were doing.

In the interest of agility and efficiency, everyone worked on everything. Trying to figure out product profitability was impossible.

If you want to drive product X harder, who do you ask? Everyone.

YOU CAN'T BRING YOUR STRATEGY OUT OF THE CLOUDS IF YOUR STRUCTURES ARE CLOUDY.

Objectives need accountability. And accountability needs transparency. Refining the structures, roles, capabilities, and ways of working in the business to align with strategy execution is crucial. Without it, the Founder has to run around being the micromanager.

You can tell others what to do but not how to do it

The gap between strategic plan and practical know-how (also known as execution) can often be the stumbling block that prevents businesses from realizing their full potential—or at least what the Founder thinks they can achieve. We've all seen it. We have a strategy; we have a goal. But then, reality hits:

EVERYONE KNOWS *WHAT* NEEDS TO BE ACHIEVED. THE REAL CHALLENGE IS FIGURING OUT *HOW* TO MAKE IT HAPPEN.

Turning a strategy into actionable change initiatives often requires a different set of skills, approaches, and perspectives than what currently exists in the business. Otherwise, you would have always done it that way from the start.

So, what happens? The manager doesn't deliver. The Founder comes across the issue again in six months (lack of transparency), gets the shits, and loses their temper. Then the Founder intervenes, like a bull in a china shop, and the execution is poor.

"This is my business. I'll do what I like."

Strategic improvement is complex. It requires planning, resource allocation, and, most importantly, an understanding of the operational intricacies involved in the journey (not just the destination).

Successful strategy execution is about more than just knowing the destination. It's about mastering the journey, one step at a time, with the right IP, skills, mindsets, tools, and flexibility to turn strategic goals into tangible, line-led results. You need to be able to change the business while running the business. And fast.

Your bright ideas aren't always valuable ideas

Change is a constant in the business world, and Founders are often quick to embrace it. But here's a thought:

> SOME CHANGE IS HELPFUL. SOME CHANGE IS VALUABLE. CHANGE THAT IS HELPFUL BUT NOT VALUABLE IS A DISTRACTION.

It's easy to get caught up in the whirlwind of opportunities, ideas ("I read this great book on the weekend"), and solutions that seem beneficial on the surface. The real question you should be asking is whether these opportunities, ideas, or solutions add genuine value to your strategic goals. And are these the *most* value-generating ideas or opportunities?

Think about a new software that might streamline a task or automate a process that may make operations smoother. These changes could be helpful, but how much do they contribute to the broader business objectives? Do they drive you closer to your strategic vision and mission, or is this just a pet project—something entertaining and fun, but only in the eyes of one individual? Is it going to suck up time, attention, and focus that could be spent on a more valuable initiative?

THE PRIMARY QUESTION HERE IS: WILL THIS IDEA HELP YOU ACHIEVE YOUR OBJECTIVES AND KEY RESULTS?

Far too many teams spend countless hours and investment on initiatives and projects that have *not been properly vetted or prioritized by a group of decision makers* in line with business strategy. They slow the business down and come at a huge opportunity cost, while those involved (often you, the Founder) ignorantly believe they are making a real difference to the business.

You struggle to run your business strategically

None of the Founders I have worked with have actually worked in, or built, a corporate. They either have little experience, or little memory, of how to manage 500-plus people to deliver a strategy and achieve a mission.

Running a bigger business involves a delicate balance between managing day-to-day operations and making changes to achieve the mission. With growth comes more people—more staff, more customers. It's easy to get caught up in the tactical grind and lose sight of the strategic priorities that really drive people toward growth and success.

This is especially true when the Founder themselves keeps getting pulled into day-to-day operations, and can't see the forest for the trees while making all the decisions for the business.

Weekly and monthly meetings are often too focused on immediate issues, operational metrics, and **looking backward**. While these tactical beats are crucial for maintaining momentum and addressing short-term challenges, they can inadvertently overshadow the strategic discussions needed to achieve big gains.

In many Founder-led organizations, strategic discussions never happen.

Over the long term, these behaviors inadvertently drive a systemic "stuck in the weeds" mentality. They don't encourage or enable managers and teams to get their heads above the water, strategically take stock, and **plan for further than a week or two ahead**.

Annual strategy offsites are simply not enough. Business is moving too fast these days; the ship sails on opportunity and value before you know it. Management operating systems need to integrate both tactical and strategic elements—including look-backs and look-forwards—so immediate tasks and long-term goals coexist and inform each other.

FOR DYNAMIC, HIGH-GROWTH BUSINESSES, "WEEKS," "MONTHS," AND "QUARTERS" ARE ARBITRARY TIME BUCKETS.

Strategically running a business requires a shift in mindset to ensure that your tactical operations support and drive your strategic vision, creating a seamless blend of action, aspiration (planning), and course correction—without you as the Founder being in the middle of it.

You never codify good performance

I've seen endless mental and emotional energy expended on poor performers in smaller businesses. However, it's always hard to put a finger on how poor their performance really is. It's equally unclear what a good performance looks like, or how staff should be doing their jobs. It isn't codified. It isn't formalized. It isn't mapped.

Founders often get fixated on what's wrong in the business, rather than taking the time to define and structurally drive what is right.

If you are constantly fighting fires, taking up the slack, and filling gaps—but not taking the time to *write down* and coach others on how *they* should fight fires, close gaps, and proactively drive good performance—you will forever be stuck as a gap filler.

This is really the root cause of all of the other factors and symptoms—the Founder being too operational. The Founder being the operating system of the business.

This creates an even bigger issue when Founders consider succession planning as the answer. *"I'll hire a COO and turn them into the CEO."* The risk of getting this wrong, hurting the business, and wasting precious time and energy is huge. You're rolling the dice on finding the right profile, personality, and smarts. You're expecting them to learn how you run your business—how to be the business operating model—in a year or two. And you're expecting to do this cheaply.

Some would call this risky. Some would call it optimistic. I would call it madness.

Proactively doing the structural work to avoid the Founder Trap will give you endlessly more insight into what your business actually needs to grow. Furthermore, if you do need a successor, you will plug them into a well-oiled machine with far greater confidence and control.

AVOIDING THE FOUNDER TRAP

You will be trapped *in* your business unless you start working *on* the business. ***This is how you avoid the Founder Trap!***

As you've just seen, running your business as a trapped Founder is complex and problematic. Driving realignment and change across so many different facets of the business, to free you as the Founder, can feel even *more* overwhelming and exhausting. And that's exactly where this all started—with exasperated Founders feeling overwhelmed, exhausted, and uninspired, and with seemingly no way out.

Well, thankfully, there *is* a way out. As I mentioned in the introduction, there is a business ecosystem—or, more accurately, a business operating system—that can get your strategy working, iterating, and capturing value without you driving it.

To implement it is a linear project. Once it's in place, and you get the ecosystem spinning, that's where business outperformance and Founder freedom lives.

This is the SHIFT™ Business Operating System.

CHAPTER 2

THE SHIFT™ BUSINESS OPERATING SYSTEM

I n this chapter, we look at the purpose and importance of a business operating system before walking through the five core elements of the SHIFT™ Business Operating System. I also reveal the key to fast and effective Founder freedom, as well as a simple tool you can utilize right now to discover your individual Founder freedom score.

WHAT IS AN OPERATING SYSTEM AND WHY IS IT IMPORTANT?

A business operating system is a structured framework of processes, tools, and practices that organizations use to manage, measure, and improve performance across all levels.

The purpose of a business operating system is to:

· Ensure that day-to-day activities, decisions, and resources are aligned with the mission and strategic objectives.

- Operate with effective business structures that foster clear lines of accountability and ownership for results, ensuring roles and responsibilities are effectively crafted and understood.

- Establish a culture of continuous improvement by systematically identifying, prioritizing, and executing improvement initiatives in line with business strategy.

- Enable informed, data-driven decisions by providing relevant information and insights to management at all levels.

- Provide a systematic approach to proactively manage, measure, and improve performance at individual, team, and functional levels.

THE FIVE CORE ELEMENTS OF SHIFT™

These five core elements make up the SHIFT™ Business Operating System:

SHIFT™ : Strategy → Harmony → Improve → Focus → Target

Applying this to medium-sized, Founder-led businesses, the SHIFT™ Business Operating System eliminates the reliance on one key person to run the business. It contains the five key structural facets of a **scalable and self-sustaining business.** This is what any business needs to be able to execute and sustain strategically aligned growth without you, the Founder, being stuck in the middle as a human operating system or puppet master.

When starting out, SHIFT™ should be implemented in a semi-linear fashion from "S" to "T" (with some parallel and overlapping elements). This can be rapidly implemented in a twelve-month program[3] to overhaul, and build up, your self-sustaining business operating system.

Once SHIFT™ is in place, it's about making the machine work and sustain itself. This is when SHIFT™ becomes a real-time, agile business

---

[3] This time frame depends on the support you've got and the state of the business. Some business coaches, with less tailored programs, aim for three years. With more intensive, hands-on support, twelve months is a good target.

IMPROVE

HARMONY   **FOCUS**

STRATEGY   **TARGET**

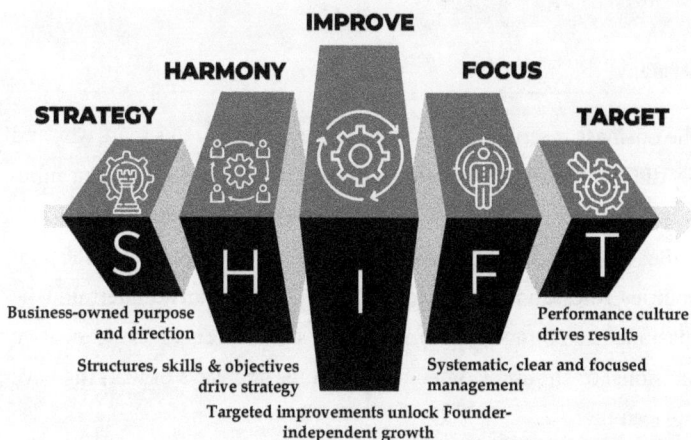

Business-owned purpose and direction

Performance culture drives results

Structures, skills & objectives drive strategy

Systematic, clear and focused management

Targeted improvements unlock Founder-independent growth

operating system that optimizes your business's ability to strategically think, execute, learn, and react—without you.

Let's go over what "good" looks like for each of the SHIFT™ elements.

Strategy

You, the Founder, have articulated what you personally want for and from the business—and this is captured in a clear Founder mandate.

Your business has a specific and clearly articulated "why"—why you do what you do, and why you are different. Your why must make sense to the customer and to the business. Your business needs to be able to deliver your why, otherwise it's just a dream. This must be articulated in a way that gives the business purpose, provides a guiding light for decision making and prioritization, and is an acid test for performance.

Your why has been distilled into an audacious medium-term **mission**—a goal to focus the troops on. This mission has been **pressure tested**—it's a stretch, but a realistic stretch—and you know the key **value drivers** that will drive success.

You have captured all of this in a **strategic story** to move hearts and minds in the business—without the need to lean solely on your charisma as the Founder!

Harmony

The business is structurally set up for success, and talks to its why and key differentiators. The strategy is cascaded across the different functions in the business, and grounded in goals and pragmatism.

Business structures directly support delivery of the strategy. Responsibilities, roles, and ways of working don't inadvertently undermine the mission. The Founder (you) isn't there to intervene, make executive decisions, or shout at someone. Structures and ways of working have replaced that.

The management team knows where to double down on capacity and capabilities—where to invest, where to have redundancy, and where they can get away with "good enough."

Functions and departments are working well together, with well-coordinated objectives and targets, to make the whole greater than the sum of its parts. This "whole" begins unlocking underlying potential that has unknowingly been bottlenecked by you, as the Founder, and prior ways of working.

Improve

No strategy or operating model is executed by just doing more of the same old stuff. The business needs a deep understanding of its core systems and processes. The business has "codified the Founder"—distilling the rainmaker magic into ways of working.

The business has a strategically prioritized hitlist of needle-moving projects or programs it is focused on. The leadership team has a roadmap and is investing in, managing, and resourcing change projects as effectively as possible.

Focus

As days turn into weeks, and weeks turn into months, the team maintains tight strategic alignment and stays the course. The management operating systems stop the team from getting sidetracked or channeling time, focus, and attention toward interesting but wasteful efforts.

The right information is escalated to the executive table and beyond. Senior management are quickly and effectively pulling strategic levers. While strategic opportunities or issues effectively make their way to the shareholder's desk (read: you) to change strategy, change the business and/or change (re)investments, you don't need to be "hanging around" to organically intercept this stuff. You have a more "grown-up" way of managing the business.

Having a structured but seamless flow of information and decision making, down and up the business, drives strategic agility, continued growth, and profitability. A tightly designed management operating system focuses the team on the most important objectives and key results.

Target

Finally, the rubber hits the road—or the customer, to be precise.

Everybody knows what their day-to-day contribution and impact needs to be. Management knows what to measure, how to measure it, and when to measure it. Managers use this information, responsibly, to drive performance and not incentivize counterproductive behaviors. They know what "good" looks like, their staff know what "good" looks like, and every individual proactively delivers that. Everyone has meaningful KPIs and targets that underpin key result delivery. A performance culture incentivizes and rewards success.

THE KEY TO FAST AND EFFECTIVE FOUNDER FREEDOM

This rounds out the holistic SHIFT™ spheres and tools your business needs to sustainably operate in a structured and deliberate way without the need of your guiding hands. With the implementation of SHIFT™ and by defining new ways of working across the spheres, you effectively distill and embed Founder IP into the business, forever. This creates a solid foundation that the team can continue to build on in a structured and controlled way, in order to live up to and exceed your Founder mandate.

The key to fast and effective Founder freedom is getting the five elements working in unison and leveraging off one another as quickly as possible to get the right stuff done, unlock value, and unlock you, as the Founder, from the business.

**THE GOAL IS TO GET YOU, THE FOUNDER, TO STOP DOING SHIFTS.
YOU NEED TO GET THE BUSINESS TO SHIFT™ *ITSELF*.**

In the remaining chapters, we'll look at each of the five elements of SHIFT™ in more detail. At this point, though, let me ask you an important question:

WHICH SHIFT™ ELEMENTS ARE YOUR BIGGEST FOUNDER-TRAPPING CHALLENGES RIGHT NOW?

If you're not entirely sure, I encourage you to utilize the **"Free the Founder" Scorecard**. By assessing the management systems and structures of your business, we'll be able to measure your Founder freedom score across the five key areas of the SHIFT™ model. In other words, you'll discover just how well your business operating system is set up to work without you.

Here's an example:

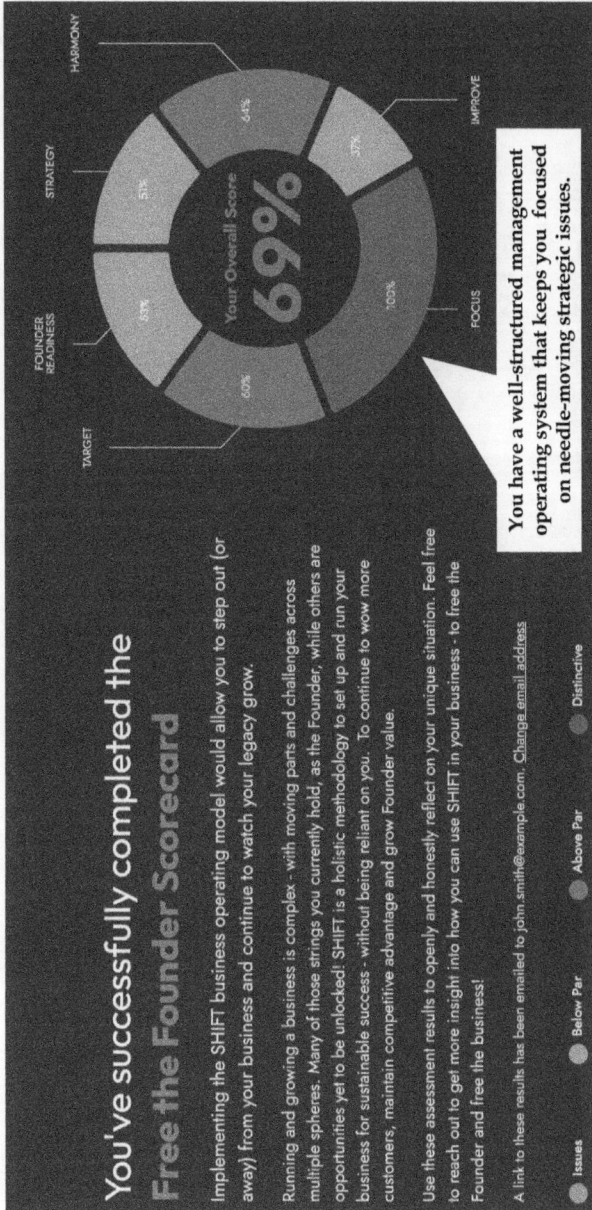

If you would like to rate your Founder freedom readiness, and get a baseline before delving into the operating system, head over to https://freethefounder.scoreapp.com/ for a free assessment.

CHAPTER 3
STRATEGY

"Anticipate. Don't improvise."

—THE KILLER (MICHAEL FASSBENDER), IN *THE KILLER* (2023)

Founders love improvising. After all, that is what built their businesses in the first place! The challenge is that many a Founder-led business could describe its strategy as "Improvise," "Follow the Founder," or "Ask the Founder."

To free a business from its Founder (and vice versa), the business needs an explicit direction to align on. While few Founder-led businesses have *needed* a strategy, it's a critical starting point to freeing a Founder. A good strategy articulates why the business exists, what makes it unique, and what significant impact it wants to achieve. Articulating your strategy is the mission-critical starting point of the SHIFT™ Business Operating System.

As you will soon see, everything hinges on strategy. Your ability to drive investments and big improvement projects. Your ability to focus your management team and ensure your team members target performance that delivers on your reason for being—the difference you make to your customers. Your ability to help the team be clear on where they are *not* focusing, building, or playing. And so on.

(For a more comprehensive, but still practical and succinct, look at strategy, please have a read of Alex M. H. Smith's *No Bullsh*t Strategy: A Founder's Guide to Gaining Competitive Advantage with a Strategy That Actually Works*.[4])

A MEANINGFUL FOUNDER MANDATE

This is a short but critical section. Many a business horror story has started without good shareholder mandates. For a Founder-owned business, being clear on what you, the Founder and owner, want to get out of it is fundamental. Any goal you set the team out to achieve will have some level of boldness and risk to it. At one end of the spectrum, you could be focused on the raising of capital and debt—high growth, high aspirations, high pressure. At the other end of the spectrum, you might have your heart set on the self-funded organic growth of a successful "lifestyle business."

Make no mistake: all businesses are hard work and a long-term game. But the capital strategy is vastly different from one business to the next. And the business strategy has to match the capital strategy—capital in and capital out.

Let's say you're the Founder of a hardware business:

---

4   https://www.amazon.com/No-Bullsh-Strategy-Alex-Smith/dp/1803136510

You may elect to continue running your hardware store on Main Street. Or, you may push the team to raise capital (and/or debt) and seek to build a nationwide home-improvement behemoth along with building and interior-design divisions. Both of these endeavors may talk to why you exist and the unique value you create for customers, but the quantum of risk and desired return is massive!

Having a very clear view from you, the Founder, of what the team should aim to achieve—and *how* you seek to extract that value from the business—is a crucial guiding light to the ongoing business leadership.

For a Founder-owned business, this means asking questions like:

· How much are you willing to reinvest for future growth (capital in)?

· How much do you want out as a minimum (capital/returns out)?

· How do you want to take it out (e.g., dividends or sell the business in ten years)?

· How much risk are you willing to attach to this plan?

Understanding the quantum of returns required, in percentage terms and in absolute dollar terms, is a tangible anchor for the current and future leadership team in owning the strategy going forward. For example, a higher-risk mandate/strategy could be:

"We have built a great foundation in the mattress market by bringing Cozy Comfy Coil mattresses to Australian customers. I want management to reinvest all profits over the next five years to launch Cozy Comfy Coil in Japan. In return, I would like 20% year-on-year growth for the next ten years. I'll extract that value from a sale of the business in ten years' time."

Depending on the Founder's (your) knowledge of the business and markets, this could be low risk or high risk. That question is best left to you as the Founder.

THE FOUNDER MANDATE QUESTION MUST BE ANSWERED TO DRAW THE LINES ON THE PLAYING FIELD FOR THE ONGOING LEADERSHIP TEAM.

Equally important is exit requirements—mechanisms and timing.

> *I worked with the owner of a successful medium-sized business. "Successful" is a loose term. Overall, the business seemed to be doing well—there were some low-profitability product lines, and there were some very profitable product lines. Was it doing well? Who knows. No one had bothered to define what "good" would look like. There were lots of other unanswered questions, like:*
>
> - *When would "the old man" retire?*
>
> - *How much would he need to retire happily? What did he want to do? What did he want to leave behind? How much would the business need to continue to support itself in his absence (that is, hiring and incentivizing a successor)?*
>
> - *How would he cash in? Would someone take over, and he take dividends? Would he look to sell the business? To what kind of buyer and at what kind of price?*
>
> - *How much risk was the Founder willing to take between now and his retirement date? HODL[5] and protect his retirement, or bet the farm and launch a new product line?*

Without having clear answers to these questions, there were absolutely no lines drawn on the field within which to play the game.

I cannot stress enough how important it is to have a clear and unified view of your Founder mandate(s), and to distill it in order to guide the management team and future strategy without you, the Founder. Clearly articulating this on a piece of paper is a very powerful process in itself.

WITHOUT THIS VALUE-RISK YARDSTICK, WHATEVER THE BUSINESS DOES WILL BE WRONG FOR SOMEONE AT SOME POINT.

Sounds simple. But teasing a clear stance out of many Founders is easier said than done. A lot of work needs to go into unpacking and understanding the business, the Founder (you), and the potential, in order to find a win-win financial goal.

---

[5] Hold On for Dear Life

It is one of your fundamental jobs as the Founder to have an educated view of what success looks like for you. This view draws the lines on the risk-and-return field in which the strategy and management team can play.

Mediating between Founders, business management, and reality is an often ongoing strategic job that is critical for maintaining healthy tension and healthy relationships. The common ground has to be distilled into a specific and meaningful Founder mandate.

A CLEAR, ALIGNED STRATEGY

Once you and your team understand what you, as the Founder, wants to get out of the business, you need to articulate a good, aligned strategy (and then a clear mission) to guide the business's leadership to deliver on your behalf.

A great strategy is deceptively simple—it's simple and impactful to read, and really hard to formulate. This is not a strategy book. Our focus here is less on determining your existential purpose and more on *distilling your strategy well so that it can be executed.*[6]

Let's start with a definition:

> STRATEGY IS A DELIBERATE POSITION IN THE MARKET, USED TO DELIVER
> A PRODUCT OR SERVICE TO A CUSTOMER, IN LINE WITH A COMPETITIVE
> ADVANTAGE, WHICH WILL SATISFY A NEED RELATIVE TO COMPETITION.

Business strategy is a view of where you are going to play and what problem you solve for your customer. It is deliberate, rich, and specific.

Mission is the medium-term goal and milestones that tell you you're on the right track and achieving success in delivering on your business and operating strategies.

Operating strategy outlines how you are going to deliver your business strategy and achieve your mission. Your operating strategy defines

---

[6] Again, see Alex M. H. Smith's *No Bullsh*t Strategy*.

how you want, and need, to build your business to go out and compete in line with your business strategy. Hence, **your business strategy explains *why* you are doing it that way.**

In my mind, a strategy answers a handful of key existential questions:

· Why do you exist? What need do you fulfill? And for whom?

· What problem do you solve? What deep pain/psychological dread do you seek to eliminate?

· Who specifically are you solving this problem for? What demographic, psychographic, industry, function, and/or subculture?

· Why are you different from other players in the market? What do you stand for that's unique? How do you serve your customers differently? What do you know/do/have that is distinctive?

Providing rich and detailed answers to these fundamental questions is difficult for many Founder-led businesses. Many just "are"—they have evolved, adapted, and stumbled upon profitability and success, but they don't have a deliberate strategic view.

Without this, the future is a gamble—especially if you, as the Founder, want to take yourself out of the equation.

I worked with a couple of Founders in the early stages of their business. In one of our first interactions, I asked, "So, what is your strategy?"

I was met with a set of bright-eyed grins and the answers, "To grow as fast as possible!" and "To take advantage of opportunities!"

That is not a strategy. You cannot build and sustain a **self-led** business around that. How do you assess your management team's plan to "take advantage of opportunities"? Where would your management team look to invest more? What new skills do they need? What projects should they prioritize? What should they say "no" to? A well-thought-out and well-articulated strategy will give your team unequivocal and *ongoing* direction on these key questions.

Your strategy outlines how you want your team to continue to be effective as a business. In most Founder-led businesses, the Founder has the strategy in the subconscious reaches of their mind. They get up every morning and give the team short-term goals and tasks. And thus, working from goal to goal, the business has evolved into what it is now.

No Founder → no (subconscious) strategy → no goals → no progress → increased risk → no business.

So, how do you articulate your strategy?

Strategic archetypes

As noted earlier, a strategy articulates the difference your business makes. You know you have to be different, and you *are* different. So, how do you formulate that difference as a strategy?

You feeling different is different to your customer feeling that you're different. And you need to be able to articulate how you *are* different, so your team knows how to *be* different! (Read it again. Trust me, it makes sense.)

Strategic archetypes are useful in doing this, as they help you define the "package deal." Defining your strategic archetype is kind of like explaining your strategic DNA. And the best way to do that is to think in differences. In other words, there has to be a continuum (also known as a range).

I did some strategy work for a petroleum retailer, which owned a bunch of gas stations. We analyzed customer trends, other competitors, size of the product segments, and growth rates. Now, strategically, they knew they were a convenience play—small-format retailer/gas station. That was a given. But it's not a strategy.

Some of the strategic choices we considered were:

- Business strategy 1: *Our middle-income customer needs an everyday item, and the stores are closed.*

Operating strategy 1: *Overstocked convenience store with a large array of "essentials" and impulse items like confectionery (think bright white lights, packed shelves, and marketing along the lines of "If you need it, we've got it").*

- Business strategy 2: *Our middle-income customer is hungry and wants to grab a quick bite while filling up in a safe, well-lit environment.*

Operating strategy 2: *Quick-service restaurant format with an anchor-brand fast-food supplier and a small selection of convenience items.*

- Business strategy 3: *Our high-income customer wants to stop for a premium coffee and a premium, freshly made lunch offering on their way to work.*

Operating strategy 3: *Coffee-shop format with a premium feel (wood accents, greenery), barista-made coffee, freshly made baguettes and other food items, and high-top wooden tables with the day's newspaper on it.*

You get the picture. Here are some examples of discrete continuums within these scenarios:

cheap | same as competition | expensive
cheap and nasty | good enough | premium
reliable | same as competition | needs repair often
convenient | same as competition | far/fragmented
quick | same as competition | slow
attentive service | same as competition | inefficient service
instant coffee | bean to cup | barista-made coffee

Whatever problem you want to solve or difference you want to make for your target customer, you have to be different from competitors and other offerings to protect your place in the market and to grow. Some of these differences are tangible (materials, quality, design, price), and some are intangible (brand, reputation, marketing, relationships, and so on).

Now, often, you can take specific sets of differences and create discrete industry archetypes, like in our petrol/convenience store example, or something like the following, which I used with one of my tech startups:

I worked with a tech business that was trying to articulate its strategic positioning. We looked at archetypes, and found three discrete "sets" of players in the market:

- *The innovators/disruptors: Driving change, breaking molds, offering cutting-edge solutions.*

- *The traditionalists: Offering old-school "backbone" solutions covering very deep but very limited functionality.*

- *The functionalists: Breaking down barriers between backbone solutions to create core business efficiency, without stepping into the "Do we need this radical innovation?" space.*

Considering solution set, history, branding, and strategy, it was useful to step back and consider these archetypes and how they related to different customer psychographics and needs. As a new entrant into the market, the team needed to decide whether to "fit into" an existing archetype so they were easier to understand, or try to establish a new archetype with the offering they were providing.

Sometimes there are multiple degrees of freedom, sometimes one or two. Generally speaking, offering and price, or segment and price, are good starting points. A two-by-two matrix can often be a useful visualization. But, again, seeing a great one makes it look easy. Building one takes insight and patience.

There is no right answer. The key here is that the team knows how you are different and where they need to invest, build, or maintain competitive advantage in order to be different and fulfill the business strategy—without you, the Founder, pulling the strings.

From archetype to "What Three Words"

An archetype should give you a more specific descriptor of the group you belong to or how you would describe yourself at a macro level. To get even more specific, you should really think about your *differentiators*. All of this comes down to positioning. How are you positioned in the market to solve a problem for a particular target customer? The more specific you can be, the more you can unequivocally guide your team.

"What Three Words" is a powerful concept in many spheres of business. (We will discuss this further in later chapters.) Fundamentally, the question you want to answer is: "What three words should our ideal customers use to describe us?"

These should be as specific and impactful as possible. The three words should both reinforce your strategic archetype and highlight how you are different to your competitors. And you should ask your customers for input. This may seem simplistic, but trust me, both the process and the end game of capturing the three words that define your business is a challenging and powerful journey.

Here are some examples:

Nike—Athletes. Innovation. Inspiration.

Reebok—Fitness. Functional. Rugged.

Microsoft—Functional. Comprehensive. Enterprise.

Apple—Design. User experience. Exclusive/premium.

From your three words to your positioning statement

Defining your three words is a useful exercise to distill how you are specifically different from your peers/competition. You will then take this a step further with a brand positioning statement (BPS) to spell out who your customers are, what value the business offers them, and how the business is different or distinctive.

Here's a template you can work off:

For (customer), who (need or opportunity),

(The department) is a (department category) that (statement of key benefit).

Unlike (competing alternative/other way of running such department)...

(The department) (statement of primary differentiation).

Corporate example: Nike

For any active human being, who is looking to improve their athletic performance and be the best self they can be,

Nike is at the forefront of sportswear and sports product design and innovation.

Unlike traditional, product-centric footwear and apparel manufacturers...

Nike strives to bring inspiration and innovation to every athlete[7] in the world.

Non-corporate example (one of my businesses): Carter

For the 21st-century new car buyer, who is looking for a convenient and efficient virtual car-buying experience,

Carter is a trusted virtual car-buying partner, helping you find, buy, and finance your perfect new car from the comfort of your living room.

Skip driving from dealer to dealer to spend your Saturday with brand-allegiant car salesmen...

Carter makes getting you into your new car easier, faster, and cheaper.

---

[7] If you have a body, you are an athlete.

The BPS is a useful framework to capture where you fit in, what you do, and how you expect the business to do it differently.

AN AUDACIOUS MISSION AND GOAL

Many companies I have worked with don't have a mission or a big, audacious goal. I think this is because many Founders and executives are *afraid* of articulating a mission and setting a goal.

DEFINING A MISSION TAKES COURAGE.

Many Founders I have worked with are afraid of articulating this because they may fail.

You may find that you don't have what it takes to deliver on those big dreams. You could overestimate your capabilities and not hit the heights you thought you would. If you can measure that failure, what does that mean about the business—or about you as the Founder, for that matter? How will the team feel about failing?

Well, the purpose of articulating your mission isn't about binary success or failure. A good mission empowers and "galvanizes" the team. A democratized strategy with a big, audacious, and specific goal drives buy-in and commitment. It drives purpose and excitement. The team aligns on stretch targets together. They aim, they shoot, and they win, or lose, together. *Either way, they grow, and they celebrate.* And they do it with or without you, the Founder.

For existing businesses with track records, existing customers, and a smart team, there is absolutely no reason to be afraid. You are sitting on value. You are sitting on distinctiveness. Your customers have chosen you and continue to choose you. Own that, understand that, and leverage that to touch more customers' lives!

The business strategy is not a goal. A goal is a milestone. A goal is a target. It's an endpoint. Google saying it wanted to achieve two million users was not a strategy; that was a goal.

A goal doesn't give a team direction on what fundamental problems to solve or how to do it. It just tells you *how many* problems you want to solve. It's an activity metric, not an effectiveness metric. A goal tells you whether you have arrived or not. *It doesn't tell you why or how you have arrived.* Strategy outlines how you are going to be effective as a business.

> **A GOAL IS A STEP. A STRATEGY IS A WAY OF BEING. TWO SIDES OF AN IMPORTANT COIN.**

Strategy isn't enough to move operations. You need to break down your strategy into missions to help you align your troops on which battle to focus on.

> **YOU DON'T TAKE OVER EUROPE (STRATEGY) BY TELLING YOUR TROOPS TO GO TAKE OVER EUROPE. YOU START WITH A SINGLE COUNTRY, A REGION, A CITY. YOU START WITH A MISSION.**

It's imperative that you take your strategy and determine a meaningful, medium-term mission to focus the troops. This should be as SMART (specific, measurable, actionable, relevant, and time-bound) as possible. This drives clarity and accountability, and allows you to objectively measure progress and success without being in the middle of the campaign.

You need to focus attention, energy, and inspiration where it matters. You need to run the business while you develop and evolve the business to maintain its edge, in line with the strategy. Being clear on a meaty mission has two key benefits:

- *It inspires.* Knowing what you are doing will have impact, and influence company strategy. This will make everyone more engaged and focused. Inspired people are happier and more productive. We all want that.

- *It makes the most use of scarce resources.* You want to make sure that you are spending time on improvements, change, and projects that really matter.

> **YOU WANT TO STRATEGICALLY PRIORITIZE YOUR TEAMS' TIME, FOCUS, AND ATTENTION. THIS INCLUDES KNOWING WHAT TO SAY "NO" TO.**

"If I spend a lot of time on X, will it help me achieve my mission? No? Well then, maybe I shouldn't spend time on that..."

A good mission should capture both your strategic intent and a medium-term goal or position from which you can measure progress.

I worked with a team in specialized insurance. Their focus was on insuring impaired lives—people with diabetes and other chronic manageable conditions.

After a thorough strategy review exercise, we finally landed on the mission statement: "Be actively changing the lives of 60,000 diabetics by 2016."

The statement captured the "actively changing" nature of the business model—keeping people healthier and enjoying a better quality of life—but it also set a target and a time frame. There was a large stadium down the road that seated around 60,000 people. We had the teams visualize that stadium full of happy, chanting clients—just like at a weekend football game.

This rallied the troops around an audacious mission directly linked to the strategy of the business. The day-to-day impact was more than anticipated. Managers used it to drive purpose. They used phrases like, "Improving your sales numbers will help us change the lives of 60,000 people by 2016." Or, "This really won't help us change people's lives and achieve '60-16,' so let's spend the time on something else."

Your mission should be aligned to your strategy *and* should be audacious. But it can't be ludicrous. I'll explain what I mean by that in the next section.

WHAT DO YOU NEED TO BELIEVE?

Let's take stock of where you are. You have a good idea of why the business exists and the problems it solves. You have a mission you want to focus on and rally the business behind. But, there is still a lot you don't know. So, before you set your team up for failure, let's think through the key value drivers of your business, how these could evolve with growth, and what you need to believe to ensure your mission has a chance of becoming a reality.

Thinking through how your specific business might grow and evolve will inevitably lead to questions and what-if scenarios. Here's an example:

"We want to double our sales of product X in the next two years.

"What if we must move to marketing channel A and our cost of customer acquisition doubles?

"What if, while we grow, our human productivity drops by 20%?

"What if a new competitor emerges and undercuts our pricing by 50%?"

It isn't enough that this be an intellectual or whiteboarding exercise. *It is important to turn these scenarios into numbers.* Before you lock in your mission and audacious goal, it is critical that you model the operational outcomes and combinations that would need to play out to make that goal achievable.

TAKE EACH OF THE KEY VALUE DRIVERS IN THE BUSINESS AND ASK YOURSELF: "WHAT DO WE NEED TO BELIEVE?"

The purpose of this is to pressure test core assumptions and business variables in a "ludicrousness test." At what point does "What do we need to believe?" to support a particular scenario become "We would have to be ludicrous"?

Building on the same example, here's how that might look:

"We will expand into country A and expect our productivity to be the same." Ludicrous.

"As we grow, our lead volumes need to triple. We are assuming our cost of customer acquisition will stay the same." Ludicrous.

So, what do you need to believe?

Take your business value drivers and build a one-page, five-year financial model with them to play out a believable future. Here's an example.

	Comments	Jan	Feb	Mar	Apr	May	Jun	Jul	Aug	Sep	Oct	Nov	Dec
REVENUE													
Inflation	3%												
Market share	50,000												
Growth rate month on month		0.50%	0.52%	0.55%	0.57%	0.60%	0.62%	0.64%	0.67%	0.69%	0.72%	0.74%	0.76%
Sales target	12 additional sales per month	250	262	274	286	298	310	322	334	346	358	370	382
Sales per workday	flex for each years growth	12.5	13.1	13.7	14.3	14.9	15.5	16.1	16.7	17.3	17.9	18.5	19.1
Number of quotes received	5% Quotes to Sales ratio	5,000	5,240	5,480	5,720	5,960	6,200	6,440	6,680	6,920	7,160	7,400	7,640
GP per sale		8,000	8,000	8,000	8,000	8,000	8,000	8,000	8,000	8,000	8,000	8,000	8,000
Insurance sales	10% Insurance sales to sales ratio	25	26	27	29	30	31	32	33	35	36	37	38
Revenue per Insurance sale	800 Rev per insurance pcd	800	800	800	800	800	800	800	800	800	800	800	800
Total revenue		2,020,000	2,116,960	2,213,920	2,310,880	2,407,840	2,504,800	2,601,760	2,698,720	2,795,680	2,892,640	2,989,600	3,086,560
Profit before tax		1,581,001	1,600,902	1,507,102	1,803,302	1,895,502	1,987,702	2,081,902	2,176,102	2,270,902	2,364,502	2,459,702	2,278,402
Total costs		438,999	516,058	706,818	509,578	512,338	517,098	519,858	522,618	525,578	528,138	530,898	808,159
COSTS													
Marketing Costs													
Digital marketing spend	10 Cost per quote	78,500	81,260	84,020	86,780	89,540	92,300	95,060	97,820	100,580	103,340	106,100	108,860
Marketing management fee	15% Agency management fee	50,000	52,400	54,805	57,200	59,600	62,000	64,400	66,800	69,200	71,600	74,000	76,400
Design and content development		7,500	7,860	8,220	8,580	8,940	9,300	9,660	10,020	10,380	10,740	11,100	11,460
Other ATL		10,000	10,000	10,000	10,000	10,000	10,000	10,000	10,000	10,000	10,000	10,000	10,000
PR		1,000	1,000	1,000	1,000	1,000	1,000	1,000	1,000	1,000	1,000	1,000	1,000
Staff - fixedish													
Executive	1,000,000	83,333	83,333	83,333	83,333	83,333	83,333	83,333	83,333	83,333	83,333	83,333	83,333
Ops Manager	250,000	20,833	20,833	20,833	20,833	20,833	20,833	20,833	20,833	20,833	20,833	20,833	20,833
Marketing analyst	150,000	12,500	12,500	12,500	12,500	12,500	12,500	12,500	12,500	12,500	12,500	12,500	12,500
Call Centre Manager	180,000	15,000	15,000	15,000	15,000	15,000	15,000	15,000	15,000	15,000	15,000	15,000	15,000
Front end developer - senior	150,000	12,500	12,500	12,500	12,500	12,500	12,500	12,500	12,500	12,500	12,500	12,500	12,500
Development Manager	180,000	15,000	15,000	15,000	15,000	15,000	15,000	15,000	15,000	15,000	15,000	15,000	15,000
Developer Snr	150,000	12,500	12,500	12,500	12,500	12,500	12,500	12,500	12,500	12,500	12,500	12,500	12,500
Developer - junior	120,000	10,000	10,000	10,000	10,000	10,000	10,000	10,000	10,000	10,000	10,000	10,000	10,000
Front end developer - junior	100,000	8,333	8,333	8,333	8,333	8,333	8,333	8,333	8,333	8,333	8,333	8,333	8,333
Additional dev, testing, and reporting	50,000	4,167	4,167	4,167	4,167	4,167	4,167	4,167	4,167	4,167	4,167	4,167	4,167
Debtors support (part time)	50,000	4,167	4,167	4,167	4,167	4,167	4,167	4,167	4,167	4,167	4,167	4,167	4,167
Finance Manager (part time)	50,000	4,167	4,167	4,167	4,167	4,167	4,167	4,167	4,167	4,167	4,167	4,167	4,167
Senior Account Manager	200,000	16,667	16,667	16,667	16,667	16,667	16,667	16,667	16,667	16,667	16,667	16,667	16,667
Staff - variable (see bottom of sheet)													
KAM support	60,000	120,000	120,000	120,000	120,000	120,000	120,000	120,000	120,000	120,000	120,000	120,000	120,000
Number of KAMs		1	2	2	2	2	2	2	2	2	2	2	2
Bonuses													272,500
Travel re-imbursements		5,000	5,000	5,000	5,000	5,000	5,000	5,000	5,000	5,000	5,000	5,000	5,000
Other costs													
Data sources	300	7,700	7,700	7,700	7,700	7,700	7,700	7,700	7,700	7,700	7,700	7,700	7,700
IT licences	500	4,500	4,800	4,800	4,800	4,800	4,800	4,800	4,800	4,800	4,800	4,800	4,800
CRM direct licensing fees		7,500	8,000	8,000	8,000	8,000	8,000	8,000	8,000	8,000	8,000	8,000	8,000
CRM added infra fees		4,400	4,400	4,400	4,400	4,400	4,400	4,400	4,400	4,400	4,400	4,400	4,400

This is not a model of broad extrapolations of a P&L. No, this is an operational driver model built up of the customer leads, sales, products, prices, materials, staff, and any other operational "thing" you need to run your business.

These are inextricably linked. To make a sale, you need a salesperson. To make one million sales, how many salespeople do you need? How fast can you recruit, onboard, and ramp them up? What do you need in order to do that fast enough? What are your conversion rates? Your scenarios of customer acquisition costs?

If you think about how the different scenarios play out, how does the business look, evolve, and grow?

MODEL IT AND DETERMINE *WHAT YOU NEED TO BELIEVE* IN ORDER TO ACHIEVE YOUR DESIRED STRATEGY AND MISSION.

I've built these models in an afternoon with Founders. The juice is in the pressure testing of the assumptions and outcomes with the senior managers of the various portfolios. In the end, your strategy and associated headline goals should be backed by reasonable assumptions of what it will take to get there, and what the key drivers of success are.

The by-product of this exercise is working with the Founder and the leadership team to get a deep appreciation of how the business works. What have we tried and seen in the past? What do we understand, and what don't we understand (even if it's just an educated guess or gut feeling)? We are effectively mapping out the moving pieces of the business and saying, "What if...?"

It's an invaluable exercise for a management team or a new senior leader, if done with intent.

AN INSPIRING STRATEGIC STORY

Once you have defined a solid strategy and determined an audacious (and pressure-tested) mission, you should communicate this in an inspiring strategic story.

This showed up beautifully just the other day, when I was preparing some 360-degree feedback for the head of a global business I was working with. I asked one of the managers, *"What could Natalie work on?"* The response was, *"She has such good ideas—a good strategy—I just wish she would write it down!"*

> **IF YOU WANT EVERYONE TO BE ON THE SAME PAGE, MAYBE YOU SHOULD START WITH A PAGE.**

A strategic story is just that. It is a one-page executive summary of where you are, where you're going, and what's important. This one-pager doesn't get discussed and then filed. This is a *narrative*, and it should be used, revisited, and revised often. It is a *working* one-pager.

> **REMEMBER: REPETITION IS A MANAGEMENT TOOL.**

People get caught up in the day-to-day. The further toward the frontline your team members are, the more they're dodging bullets and digging trenches. It's easy for them to forget what war they're fighting when they are mentally so far from home. Your strategic story ties this together. It provides the "why" and the "what." It gives a succinct narrative of where you are and what you're doing next.

Here's an example of a go-to-market strategic narrative:

"We are a banking AI solutions specialist. We leverage our deep financial services expertise and experience to be the leading AI technology partner in banking, shaping and delivering AI roadmaps that drive distinctive customer experience, efficiency, and security for our clients.

"Our strategic focus for 2024 has been taking our new generative AI product to market. Focus has been on the banking sectors in Germany, the US, and Canada. The first half of the year saw great interest from existing clients, sales partners, and high-priority prospects.

"As the sales cycles have evolved, it has become clear that we need integrations into third-party software solutions that are different from the standard integrations of our core product. Building these will require different expertise and resources, and may introduce IP risk.

"We are setting up a cross-functional hit squad to build and orchestrate our third-party integration and partnership strategy. This will be completed by end of October to inform our AI strategy for 2025, and give us time to engage partners and clients on the outcomes.

"This will position us well to be actively shaping the AI journeys of 50% of the major banks in Germany, the US, and Canada by the end of 2025."

As I said, your strategic narrative should be a **succinct one-pager** of what your strategy is, what your next mission is, and what the business's short-term focus areas should be. It will bring richness and logic to your strategic positioning, and help the team **maintain alignment**. They can also engage with you and easily update it as things evolve.

The strategic story will help you inspire your team. It adds depth and understanding around *why* what they are doing is purposeful—especially when you aren't there to remind them.

As I said at the start of this chapter, articulating your strategy is the mission-critical starting point of the SHIFT™ Business Operating System. Now it's time to explore the second element of the system: **HARMONY**.

STRATEGY TO-DO LIST

☐　You have a clearly articulated "why," strategy, and mission that are business-owned. The team is committed to the business strategy and vision, not you as the Founder.

☐　You have a specific and meaningful Founder mandate that details the quantum of returns and timing of these returns expected by you, as well as the reinvestment intent.

☐　You have categorized your strategic archetype, so you are clear on what kind of player you are in your industry.

☐　Your "What Three Words" give specific guidance on what you deliver to your customer, and your brand positioning statement takes this a step further to expand on how you are different from your competitors in your category.

☐　You are targeting a SMART (specific, measurable, actionable, relevant, and time-bound) mission. It is audacious, but you know what it will take to get there and how your business value drivers need to evolve to support the mission.

☐　You've wrapped this up and captured this in a compelling strategic story to engage the hearts and minds of the team.

CHAPTER 4
HARMONY

*"A successful team is a group of
many hands but of one mind."*

BILL BETHEL

L et's kick off this chapter with a quick musical analogy. If you are missing a percussion section in your orchestra, or if your percussion section is weak, it will impact the symphony. If you have a flutist sitting with the double basses (opposite all the other flutists), the symphony will sound off. If your orchestra is given the title of the symphony but no sheet music—well, that would be interesting.

In the same way, let's see how well your orchestra (your business) is set up for success—and how you can help it operate without you, the Founder, as the conductor!

How *harmoniously* is your business set up to deliver on your strategy and mission, as outlined in the previous chapter? And how well is it set up without you, the Founder, filling in gaps?

Strategy and strategic thinking should happen at all levels of the organization. Most of the frustration I see in Founders and corporate executives alike comes from their teams not focusing on priorities, or the stuff that will really move the needle. And a lot of this comes from business structure, leadership, and not cascading a sense of strategic thinking. If a Founder isn't going to be around to keep the herd moving in the right direction, cascaded strategic structure, direction, and focus are critical.

The way your business is structured can inadvertently upset or undermine strategic focus. The capabilities and capacity you invest in can help or hinder your business. Even if you have the right people in the right place, they need to know what to focus on and how to work effectively as part of the team. As Bill Bethel said, *"many hands, one mind."*

YOUR OPTIMAL BUSINESS BLUEPRINT

Your business structure is a choice. It can actually be a radical choice that materially changes how your business thinks and works together. Along with your strategy, you should take stock of your options and scenarios when it comes to structuring your business.

Your business structure, or business blueprint, is different from your "organizational structure." It isn't people-centric—rather, it focuses on the important parts and pieces of a business. If a person features, then you have a sustainability and risk problem!

Your optimal business blueprint is answered with questions like: "What are your product lines?" "What is their profitability?" "What are your regions?" "Are you one business, or a combination of multiple small businesses?" Your structures will drive groupthink around "how the business works" and what is important. Business structure can drive collaboration. It can drive focus. It can also drive silo mentality, confusion, and distraction.

Considering your strategy and where you are in its evolution, you should choose a company structure to match.

I worked with a small tech company that had several products and services. In the interests of economies of scale and resource efficiency, they ran the business very fluidly. Management and staff worked across products and services in very much an "on demand" way.

A strategic review unpacked the profitability of the various products and services, and we found there was a significant difference. Doing a profit pools analysis, one "service line" had significant growth potential and profitability, while another was very low margin and very saturated and competitive. One product was complex, with more challenging growth potential, but still very profitable. Another was a "no-brainer" that was easier to sell and in demand.

We restructured the company into multiple sub-companies, clustering service lines more deliberately for growth, each with its own P&L and leadership. With renewed clarity and focus, and more tailored P&L control, the high-potential service lines immediately started to achieve over 25% year-on-year growth rates, sustaining this for over five years.

Before drawing boxes and lines on a page, it is helpful to take stock of the evolution of your business as a whole, and how your business structure does (or does not) talk to your current strategy, opportunities, and focus areas. Then, map out what the optimal business blueprint could look like. How could the products, service lines, and functions of your business fit together? Is there a clear and elegant solution relative to your strategy? What are the scenarios and trade-offs? Should you consider changing anything?

As an example, below is a strategic view from the life insurance business I mentioned in the introduction to this book. After a strategy and value driver assessment, we felt it best to align the functions and departments in the business around four key functions, each with similar objectives in the customer value chain.

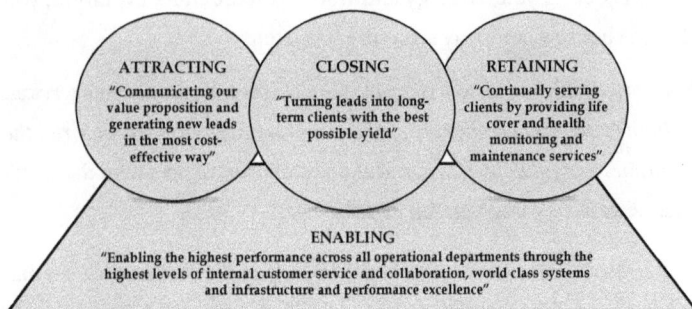

We then appointed a leader for each of these four facets of the business, who would be responsible for driving the right subcultures and strategic business objectives for their respective business pillar.

OBJECTIVES AND KEY RESULTS

Now that you have articulated why you exist, where you are going, and how you should think about the pieces of the business, you need to get tactical. Specifically, you need to make sure the various pieces of the business are focused on **the right outcomes to achieve the mission and deliver the strategy.**

Objectives and key results (OKRs) have been around for over fifty years, but I still come across many managers and executives who have never heard of them. (If you *are* familiar with OKRs, feel free to skip this section, which will cover the essentials. There is also some great, comprehensive content out there, including examples.)[8]

OKRs drive focus. I have been in numerous work environments where staff are snowed under and running from one focus area to the next, making them very inefficient. In most cases, there isn't even a clearly defined strategy—but you must appreciate that a strategy and a

---

[8]   https://www.whatmatters.com

mission are broader guideposts. They don't directly link to what I am doing right now.

> **OKRs CLOSE THE GAP BETWEEN STRATEGY AND DAY-TO-DAY WORK IN A VERY PRIORITIZED WAY.**

In a nutshell, OKRs are broken down like this:

Strategic objective 1: Clearly defined goal

- *SMART key result 1.1*
- *SMART key result 1.2*
- *SMART key result 1.3*

Strategic objective 2: Clearly defined goal

- *SMART key result 2.1*
- *SMART key result 2.2*
- *SMART key result 2.3*

The best OKRs visual I have seen is of a road winding through hills. The objective is where you want to end up—the medium-term goal. The key results are the steps and milestones that get you to that goal. Setting out OKRs is prioritized strategic planning.

OKRs – Objectives & Key Results

Q4
End 202X

Key Result 5

Key Result 2
Key Result 3

Objective

Q3

Specific
Measurable
Action-oriented
Relevant and realistic
Time-bound

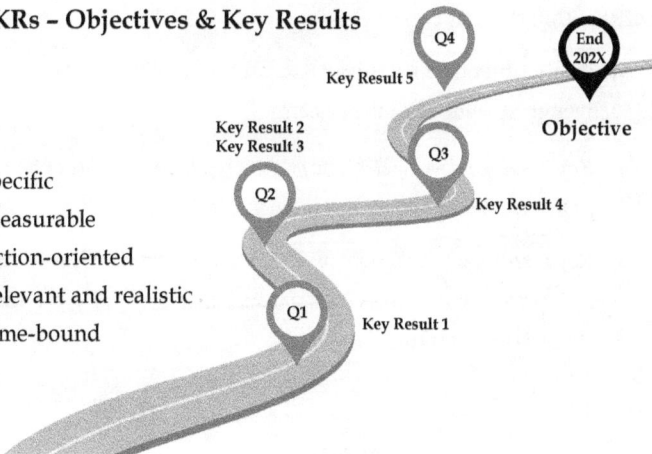

Q2

Key Result 4

Q1

Key Result 1

Also, OKRs *cascade*. You start with your strategy and mission. You then set OKRs at an executive level, then a senior manager level, then a manager/department level, and so on. This way, you have a cohesive and aligned set of OKRs that roll up to support your strategy.

Starting with your business strategy, you consider your mission and your key value drivers. You set three to five executive- or business-level OKRs. You then cascade these to ensure cohesion. I like to take a top-down approach by taking the business mission and OKRs and thinking through the following questions with each manager:

Given our strategic narrative and mission, what are the three to five objectives for the year that will move the needle for the value drivers in your sphere of influence?

If you could only do three things this year to make a big difference to our performance and how we work, what would those three needle-moving things be?

I push for three to drive focus, and then we end up with four or five. We then break down the shorter-term scenario planning and plans, and distill those into key results that are SMART.

As an example, I was supporting the ramp-up of a new strategic projects lead in a $30-million, 500-person business. We developed their OKRs within the first two weeks:

Strategic objective 1: Deliver $20 million in value by December (deliver great value-adding projects)

- **Key result 1.1:** *Deploy strategic projects resources on value-optimizing projects to deliver $20 million in savings in H2.*

- **Key result 1.2:** *Develop and maintain sufficient initiatives in the strategic projects roadmap as a leading indicator to fulfilling the overall strategic projects target.*

- **Key result 1.3:** *Develop project performance management framework, with leading and lagging indicators, to drive and assess quality, on-time delivery, and efficiency of projects by August 2024.*

- **Key result 1.4:** *Leverage technology to simplify the operating model and drive efficiency.*

Strategic objective 2: Establish a strategic projects center of excellence (set up a great function)

- **Key result 2.1:** *Publish a strategic projects playbook, and train all strategic projects staff and people leaders on new ways of working by end of August.*

- **Key result 2.2:** *Implement a prioritization framework and idea funnel by end of August.*

- **Key result 2.3:** *Define and deliver a strategic projects roadmap by end of September.*

- **Key result 2.4:** *Define matrix interfaces and how to support CI staff embedded in the line by end of August.*

Strategic objective 3: Operate with a strong performance culture (build and retain a high-performing team)

- **Key result 3.1:** *Develop a strategic projects team performance management framework.*

- **Key result 3.2:** *Recognize and reward top performers to retain top talent.*

- **Key result 3.3:** *Upskill all team members to effectively and efficiently deliver work by end of October.*

- **Key result 3.4:** *Deploy resources on value-optimizing projects to maximize monetary value per FTE.*

- **Key result 3.5:** *Instill a culture of sustainable line-led change through collective problem solving, and engagement with customers and stakeholders, to drive adoption, value, and sustainable solutions.*

For each of these bullet points, I want to identify how I will know that something has been achieved or not, very transparently. What is the number and target, or what is the deliverable and date? Then I know whether that key result has been achieved, and if it has been achieved on time. I can assess the outcomes by knowing that my key results have been achieved, and, therefore, I'm fulfilling my objectives.

Because OKRs are short and succinct—at a maximum, one page or a single slide—they should be easy to remember, can be pulled up in monthly meetings, and can be put up at people's desks.

OKRs are a great tool to cascade strategy. They communicate and align strategic priorities in a structured way. The team will check in on key result progress monthly. They should have a strategic review and reflect on strategy and all OKRs quarterly (more on this in Chapter 6).

Managing distractions

A big part of OKR conversations is what is **not a priority**. There are a lot of things you *could* do this year and quarter, but you can put those on a wish list and only structurally consider them once you know your OKRs are on track, and you have capacity.

REMEMBER: TIME, FOCUS, AND ATTENTION ARE FINITE RESOURCES.

If a new major idea or project pops up, which OKR does it put at risk? Or, which OKR are you taking off the list?

There may also be a couple of projects or initiatives currently on the go that are distracting the team from important OKRs. These should be stopped!

DISTRACTION
DISTRACTION

The more you have to juggle, to think about, to plan for, to resource, the less gets done. You need to use your OKRs, every week and every month, to eliminate *distraction* and drive *action* to move your key results forward.

Now that you understand how you should think about your business (your business blueprint) and what is important for the business to achieve in the next twelve months (your OKRs), you can assess how your people, capabilities, and values are set up for success.

YOUR BUSINESS HEATMAP

Now, you need to get a handle on how well you are geared up to get there. Capacity and capabilities are a function of the people, processes, and technology in your business. Technology plays an ever more important role in how you can increase capacity through automation, self-service, and AI.

A good way to get a strategic view of your capacity and capabilities is by using a business heatmap. Take all the functions in your business—even gaps or empty ones—and put them across the top of a page. Then, as a row, place your different levels of staff, processes, systems, and any other cross-cutting core competencies you want to heatmap. Then, rate each block.

For reference, I've included below an example of a one-page executive heatmap. You'll see that I use Harvey balls with definitions that I find useful and intuitive. Having a whole page of amber dots or "three out of five" ratings doesn't help anyone.

Legend:
- ○ No resource, no function
- ◔ Ineffectively resourced
- ◑ Functioning with basic gaps
- ◕ Functioning, enroute to sustainability
- ● Effective, sustainable functionality

Row categories: Comments · Systems · Processes · Client Insights · Frontline staffing · Middle Mgmt · Senior Mgmt · Executive

Column functions: Brand · Marketing · Sales · Cust Support · Collect · Support 2 · Claims · Partners · Projects · IT Infra · IT Development · MIS · Bus. Intel and Analysis · Product Innov. · Finance · HR

Comments:

- Recent Brand Strategy launched and underway
- Potential to move to Head of Brand and Head of Direct Campaign Management without an Exec role over both
- Need a Campaign Management custodian at the Snr Mgmt level
- 2.0 intensely state. Focus on continuous improvement
- Improved CRM system required for client management, staff management and reporting
- Operations Manager needed
- This function will need senior staffing and restructuring if distribution strategy requires greater agent / broker presence
- Require a replacement for Mobil and Senior Project Associate to run high value projects
- Senior infra Mgmt gap needs to be filled
- Senior Business Analyst skills need required to round out team
- Management capacity / skills need investment. Exec level oversight gaps
- Reporting to CIO due to lack of CIO capacity
- Potential need for CIO role to house Dev, MIS, BI and BA
- Senior level "Product Executive" role vacant. Product Innovation Associate and Product Analytics Associate roles being resourced and shaped in CI1
- Potential book keeper
- SA Finance Director position required
- HR Manager straddling middle and senior management roles

A BUSINESS HEATMAP SHOULD GIVE YOU CLEAR GUIDANCE ON WHERE YOU SHOULD WORRY AND WHERE YOU SHOULDN'T.

A full Harvey ball never equals "best in the world." That's a pointless measure. "Good enough to be effective and not have to worry about for the foreseeable future" is a great shade of green in my books.

Looking at the heatmap example, you can see a couple of things quite intuitively:

- Functional gaps where the entire column is blank—partner management and focused product innovation.

- Clear leadership gaps at different levels depending on the function—this doesn't show any particular underinvestment trend in intermediate management, but rather evolutionary outcomes.

- A universal gap in customer insights across functions—something that may be worth investing in as a center of excellence to help empower the lines.

- Core systems are looking good. Some investment in secondary systems is needed.

- Processes are generally good and not cause for concern in core business areas.

A business heatmap is a powerful analytical tool, and a powerful communication and collaboration tool to use with your leadership and management team.

Actively and thoughtfully working through OKR-setting with your teams—watching them strategically problem-solve and unpack what is and what isn't working at a strategic level—can give you a ton of deep insight into your business heatmap.

Organizational structure

It's important to loop back to your business blueprint and take stock of how your organizational design does or does not reinforce how you *should* think about your business as a strategic machine. Your org design—especially the top couple of layers—is a big enabler of strategy and focus in the business.

> **HAVING THE RIGHT LEADERS IN THE RIGHT ROLES TO SUPPORT AN OPTIMAL BUSINESS BLUEPRINT DRIVES OPTIMAL STRATEGIC FOCUS, TRANSPARENCY, AND ACCOUNTABILITY.**

It's always an art to try and trade off what roles you need, and what they should look after, versus the capabilities you have in the team. Best-practice and "perfect world" org charts are worth considering to push the thinking and ask the tough questions, but at the end of the day you often must do the best you can with what you've got, or what you can find and afford.

The biggest challenge I see in Founder-led businesses is the Founder's tendency to cluster too many important things under one or two people they can trust. These individuals are generally coping, but are definitely not doing justice to the many different pieces of their portfolios.

The other challenge is being cognizant of the profile of the individual. You need to ensure their skills, capacity, *and* personality suit the work and the team.

Again, circling back to your strategy sphere, what are your priority strategic-focus areas? In your scenarios and "What do you need to believe?" analyses, where are the biggest risks, or the areas where you simply have to overinvest to make sure you get stuff right?

When you consider spans of control, responsibilities, role grades and so on, as far as reasonably possible you want to drive single-point accountability *and* single-point focus in these core strategic areas. Consider the following example:

I worked in a B2C sales business. Marketing used a number of different channels, of varying costs, to bring leads into the business. Very quickly, we saw the usual finger-pointing between sales and marketing, with sales saying, "The leads are shit," and marketing saying, "Your salespeople are shit."

With a high-growth strategy, getting under the skin of lead quality and reliable cost of customer acquisition data was critical. So, we put an entire department into the divide. The thinking was that sales should be solely focusing their selling skills on viable/warm leads. Every minute a sales-person spent on a lead that simply could not qualify for the product was a wasted minute.

We put in a lower-cost and lower-skilled "pre-qualifying" department. This team's sole responsibility was to reach a lead (that is, they are in a position to have a conversation) and ask three pre-qualifying questions. If successful, the hot lead was transferred to the sales department.

This operating strategy removed noise from the system, and drove single-point accountability and focus. It was a huge success.

From senior management to team leaders, working through "who worries about what" will give you a good idea of where your structures are driving complexity rather than clarity. Looping back to your value drivers that you thought through in your strategic modeling, who is responsible for the big, hairy, sensitive value drivers?

Now, I realize that you can't have a single senior manager for each important thing. However, you can control how much you load each portfolio—and you can certainly address where you have too many people worrying about the same thing, and thus diluting focus and accountability.

And you will get it wrong! Like everything, you take a stab, and you learn. It's helpful to have a plan B for when you become overloaded. Being proactive and deliberate about it is equally important.

"Tom, we aren't sure if this area is going to grow slowly or explode. If it explodes, we will need to find another home for it, so that you don't have too much on your plate. When and if this happens, it's by design and not a reflection of your ability to manage!"

CULTURE = VALUES AND BEHAVIORS

You may have expected this section to come up earlier. One of the biggest areas to navigate and shape is business culture. There will be change and, yes, there should be change. The culture needs to be shaped accordingly.

Famous serial entrepreneur Daniel Priestley made a key point when he said:

> **"YOU NEED TO HAVE A CORE TEAM WHO ARE LOYAL TO THE BUSINESS—NOT TO THE FOUNDER."**

So, a Founder-centric culture needs to be shifted to a business-centric culture. *And you only know what kind of culture the business needs once you know what the business needs to achieve, and what it needs to look like (strategy and harmony).*

With capabilities and capacity, you need to focus on the culture to support the business strategy and drive performance. Culture = values and behaviors.

Values

The difference between values and behaviors is nuanced, but important.

Values are the core beliefs or principles that guide and motivate attitudes and behaviors. They serve as a foundational compass, helping to dictate what is important and worthwhile. Values are more abstract and *are not always directly observable.*

Values influence decision-making processes, prioritize what is important, and shape the overall organizational culture. They are more about the "why" behind actions—why something is done, why it is valued, and so on.

In my opinion, there are silly company values and there are crafty company values. Here are some examples:

Silly company values: *"Honesty, integrity, and respect."* *These should be a core part of an employment contract. They shouldn't need to take up space as company values.*

Crafty company values: *"Accountability, legacy, connection, fulfillment, resilience."* *Crafty company values don't just reinforce basic, expected values. They pull out those distinctive values that are important in delivering your desired impact as an organization and operating differently from your competitors.*

Crafting company values that elicit the right kinds of mindsets and behaviors to drive the culture you want to foster is what the exercise is all about. Articulating what people should already be or display in order to be employed and paid a salary (being honest, for example) is a waste of time, in my opinion.

Engaging the team and revising the company values—in light of the strategy and OKRs—is a great way to symbolically support the "Free the Founder" initiative and get the team rallied around and shaping a new era or chapter of positive change. I've run many creative workshops with teams to unpack what day-to-day values, attitudes, and behaviors drive progress in the business. I've run carefully designed surveys to crowdsource input and tease out nuances specific to the business, its customers, and its competitors. With a bit of thinking, it's a quick and fun process that elicits great results, with a lot of energy and buy-in from the team.

And, with your values (internal), you also articulate behaviors (external).

Behaviors

Behaviors are the observable and measurable actions and manners exhibited by individuals. They are the manifestation of underlying values and beliefs in real, visible conduct. They are more about the "what" and "how"—what someone does, and how they approach reality.

So, directly linked to your values are the behaviors and characteristics you want to see every day. Considering your functional strategy and OKRs, do you need people to be fast-moving and 80/20? Analytical and cautious? Operate with emotion and compassion? Prioritize "resilience" in a high-change environment?

What you want to see (behaviors) and why you want to see it (values) will help you be deliberate about who you hire, the behaviors you foster, and the actions you recognize and reward. Part of this is engaging with the team to tease these out. Ask yourselves:

> *What kinds of people are successful here? What kinds of people could we use more of? What kinds of people don't fit in here?*

These are amazing questions to formally and holistically unpack with the remaining team and get them co-creating the future of the business that they are allegiant to. In one business I worked with, I collaborated with all the staff to revise the values of the business as the team came together under new leadership. These were the results:

Be bold!

- *We are all hand-picked industry imposters. We're using our intrinsic skills and deep industry knowledge to do great things.*

- *Maintain a level of responsible fearlessness. Punch above your weight.*

- *Back yourself. We back you.*

- *We are all in the deep end together. Learn to swim. Fail fast and learn quick.*

Don't be an arsehole

- *"Chop wood. Carry water." Be a good human. Be humble and mindful.*

- *We are a group of humble scalers. We chase greatness with humility.*

- *Understand yourself and others. Be your authentic self while going with the flow.*

- *Don't take yourself too seriously. Get loose, laugh, and be funny. Have a sense of humor.*

Be the change

- *Don't just be. Be something.*

- *Work with feeling and spirit. Be passion-inspired. We don't just make change—we inspire change.*

- *"See one. Do one. Teach one." Be a sponge! But don't just learn to swim—teach someone else how to. Here, everyone's a coach.*

- *We are open and honest. We value transparency. Don't beat around the bush, but always act with kindness.*

Be a team

- *We chop wood and carry water together. Collaborate with heart.*

- *"If you're not sure whose job it is, it's yours." We are a small, tight, flat team. We work better with all hands on deck.*

- *We recognize and celebrate great contributions. We recognize how we do things as importantly as the outcomes we achieve.*

- *We are a family. Back your team. Every thought and every perspective counts.*

Be a builder

- *Here you can have great impact. Own it! Take responsibility and be accountable. Leave things better than you found them.*

- *Be deliberate. Do things on purpose. Know the "why" in everything you do.*

- *Roll up your sleeves—don't wait around for things to happen. Do your work. Do it conscientiously. And keep it simple.*

- *We are builders, not runners. We design our way of doing things, and only perfect it through trial and error. Focus on the task with a view of the future.*

Company and functional cultures are a strong reflection of management, and of the characteristics and behaviors you look for and encourage. So, *leadership style* is an important starting point. More on this in the next section.

YOUR LEADERSHIP HEATMAP

Next to your business heatmap, you need a leadership heatmap. You need to make sure you have the right senior crew on your ship. There are five key elements I like to assess when looking at a management team:

- Role requirements and OKRs

- Leadership style and Enneagram/personality profile

- Skill

- Will

- Values and behaviors

It is important to remember that people don't change. As much as you may want your star business development manager to grow into a great managing director in six months, it's risky and unlikely. Having an honest and objective view of the leadership of the business without you as the Founder, and pinpointing structural and systematic ways of supporting the team, is critical.

> YOU CAN HAVE AMAZING MANAGERS WITH POOR STRUCTURE. YOU CAN HAVE AMAZING STRUCTURE WITH POOR MANAGERS. YOU *CANNOT* LEAVE THE BUSINESS WITH POOR MANAGERS *AND* POOR STRUCTURE.

Developing the right structure to support the leadership team—amazing or poor—starts with an objective and thorough leadership heatmap.

I would strongly recommend *not* doing this in a dark room all by yourself. Firstly, you are emotionally connected to your leadership team and have your own built-in biases. Secondly, using a sounding board to unpack, discuss, and hold up a mirror is very important—preferably, a sounding board that can prompt you with thought-provoking questions pertinent to your business and the roles being discussed. A sounding board that has worked with a variety of businesses and managers. This enables a more holistic and honest assessment.

Role requirements and OKRs

Sounds obvious. However, I have worked with *so* many senior managers in Founder-led businesses that are there because they are "nice guys," or because they were promised something ten years ago during a totally different era of the business.

You need to start with what *role* the business needs (for example, a product manager) and the subsequent OKRs for the next twelve months (in this case, the OKRs are based on where product management is in its maturity). Then, you assess the person in the context of the role requirements—not vice versa!

Leadership style and personality profile

In my first book, *From Manager to Executive*, I go into detail on personality profiling, leadership styles, and leadership stories. In the context of *Exit without the Exit*, it is important to match leadership style to the objectives and culture you need to nurture in the business. If you need to tighten up operations, drive a transformation, and foster the associated accountability and discipline, you may need more of an autocratic leadership style at the helm.

If it is a services business and you, the Founder, have a loving and caring nature, you need to foster a facilitative leadership style to stay the course.

Think about what the business needs to achieve its mission and OKRs!

Considering your executive heatmap—and, importantly, any correlations with your management's characteristics and blind spots—may be the key to unlocking performance. Otherwise, there can be a disconnect, as the personal example below highlights.

I have a strong, authoritative leadership style. I thrive in high-growth, transformative environments like early-stage startups, rapid scale-ups, and turnarounds and performance transformations involving significant re-engineering.

For my sins, I was an operations manager in the early days of my career. Building and growing a bunch of departments, managers, and teams that reported to me, something strange started to happen over a three-year period. My managers started to miss the details. I really focus on the 80/20 big picture, and hate micromanaging. That means that I don't go into the details unless there is a dire issue that warrants it. In the general course of business, my 80/20 focus had imprinted on the team and they started to let finer details slip. Over time, these started adding up to become significant blind spots.

You can imagine the gear change and shock when I hired a replacement ops manager who was a lot more detail-oriented and fastidious. The pendulum had swung, and my managers were grumpy. Oh well, such is life/business.

I try to remember the old adage:

> **"WHAT INTERESTS MY MANAGER FASCINATES ME."**

In the context of your strategy and OKRs, it is imperative to understand what leadership styles will be left behind when you remove yourself as the Founder. How will these shape the business and the culture? Does this need to be influenced in any way?

I would always strongly suggest running a well-thought-through, and non-anonymous, *360-degree feedback process*. This will give far more holistic and honest input into leadership styles and culture.

The non-anonymous part ensures accountability and transparency. It also provides rich and valuable insights that can be used for internal communications and one-on-one change management with key staff members.

Using an external facilitator to safeguard the process is always encouraged for 360-degree feedback.

Skill

For skill, you need to consider both hard operational skills (such as product marketing, software development, and management accounting) as well as strategic and continuous improvement skills (such as abstract reasoning and strategic planning, business analytics, and business process optimization).

In some cases, you will want to hire for the skills and experience you need (or rent a specific consultant). Or, you may want to deeply invest in targeted skills development programs, in the context of your strategy execution process. Either way, it is imperative to know what skills you have where, and be conscious and deliberate about any gaps or investments you should make.

Will

Will is certainly subjective. I would, again, go back to 360-degree feedback and determine whether this leader/manager is an energy giver or an energy taker. How long have they been with the business? Are they getting itchy for challenges that are outside the scope of the business? Are their personal motivations and aspirations aligned with the business strategy?

Values and behaviors

Can the leader/manager in question "walk the talk"? Once you know what values and behaviors are most important for your journey over the next one- to two-year period, ask yourself: How much has this leader/manager been able to demonstrate and role model the desired behaviors we need from the broader team? Can they coach and support team members on living up to the values?

Synthesis

I include an overall synthesis score to capture the outcomes of the assessment or discussion. I like to use a score out of ten. In my experience, anything below an eight is cause for concern. I don't know why—it just works out that way. Try it.

As you can see in the following example:

- Mark is a rock star. Given his broad operational portfolio, this is definitely a good sign.

- Andrew and Mike are cause for concern. You need clear improvement plans or interventions here. Their leadership styles, values and behaviors, and wills all point to them being the wrong kinds of leaders for this stage of the business and team.

- Maria needs some motivation or incentives.

Legend:
- ◕ Material issues
- ◑ Needs attention
- ◕ Good enough
- ● A real strength

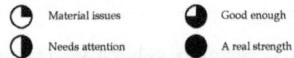

Name	Role	Leadership style	Ennea	Skill	Will	V&B	Synth
Mark	GM	Authoritative / Autonomous	8	●	●	●	10
Carmen	BDM	Task-oriented / Directive	1/3	◕	●	●	9
Maria	CMO	Democratic	8/4	●	◑	◕	8
Andrew	CTO	Facilitative	2/5	◐	◐	◔	4
Nicole	Projects	Charismatic / Transformational	7	◕	●	●	9
Mike	Customer Success / Support	Democratic / Laissez-faire	5	●	◑	◕	6
Michelle	Product	Participative / Facilitative	5/4	◕	●	●	9

SETTING UP FOR HARMONIOUS SUCCESS

Firstly, yes, these are not "scientific assessments"—these are strategic assessments. There is no perfect scoring or assessment tool, and there shouldn't be. You are considering the strategic future of a real business in an imperfect world. By completing the harmony assessment, you'll gain a much deeper understanding of the strengths and weaknesses within your team, and the opportunities and trade-offs.

Taking a big step back, you need to assess:

- Your OKRs and what is key to moving the needle for the business in the next twelve months.

- Your business blueprint and business heatmap, and where you have the most work to do across people, processes, and systems.

- Your org structure and leadership heatmap, and where the business is well-led versus where you have some hotspots.

Putting these next to each other, you'll be able to holistically assess where you can continue with what you have got, where you need to make some responsibility changes, and where you need to potentially hire and fire.

This is a critical "clean up shop" step in setting the business up for harmonious, self-sustaining success. Further to that, you cannot underestimate the importance of internal communication, as well as role modeling and leadership development.

Internal communication

Change management is key, both when freeing a Founder and when driving significant strategic changes in how the business works. You want your leadership and staff to be fired up, bought in, and contributing to your business evolution.

In my experience, small to medium businesses don't take a structured approach to communication. I'm not advocating "comms for the sake of comms"—rather, I'm just stressing the importance of having a communication strategy. You are now in a perfect position to develop one. You have refined your strategy, you have developed OKRs, and you have a view that big, exciting changes are coming.

IMPENDING CHANGE WITHOUT COMMUNICATION AND SPECIFICS DRIVES ANXIETY AND MISTRUST OVER BUY-IN AND EXCITEMENT!

Having an honest, meaningful, and exciting communication strategy allows you to clearly communicate what is happening, when it is happening, and *why* it is happening. And you communicate this from all directions, across any and all available communication channels.

Now, it must be said that very few people are actually that good at structured communication and copywriting. Capturing your strategic narrative in plain but specific and emotive language is an art. Articulating your Founder aspirations for the business, and how you are going to be stepping back to "unleash" the power of the team, is an art. Developing catchphrases for your OKRs, which capture the essence of the work to be done but add an element of hype and purpose, is an art. Designing the right symbolism and iconography to match your strategy and OKRs is an art.

An art that is worthwhile to create buy-in, comfort, focus, and excitement. It's a fair amount of work, and it takes a particular personality profile to do it justice. And, in my opinion, it's worth the investment.

Not only is good internal communication very impactful and exciting, it's "grown up." It symbolizes "company" versus "business." Not only will it support your "Free the Founder" efforts, but it will also symbolically encourage everyone to step up and grow up. (We'll discuss this in more detail in Chapter 6.)

Role modeling and leadership development

Credibility starts and stops with your people-leader team. If you, as the Founder, are driving messaging and change, but there isn't visible buy-in and change at your people-leader level, it does more harm than good. It can turn your strategy and efforts into something to fear and fight against.

YOUR KEY CHANGE AGENTS ARE YOUR PEOPLE LEADERS.

You need to leverage your leadership heatmap and arm your leaders with the right ammunition (skills, strategic insight, change insight, talking points, and behaviors) to go out and lead the charge with their people.

Bringing them along the strategic and OKR journey is key to getting buy-in and fostering conviction. OKRs, clear values and behaviors, and *clear messaging and "sound bites"* enable the management team to lead in their own authentic way in monthly meetings, weekly standups, and daily interactions.

ONCE AGAIN: REPETITION IS A MANAGEMENT TOOL.

Conditioning comes from repetition and routine. Your job is to hold your people leaders accountable for being the change and driving the change, so that new ways of working (behaviors) take hold.

You should be using semi-annual 360-degree feedback to get a gauge on how well your leaders are doing. From there, you can drive specific leadership development initiatives to take them from good to great.

Now that we have covered "Strategy" and "Harmony," it's time to proceed to the third element in the SHIFT™ Business Operating System: *IMPROVE.*

HARMONY TO-DO LIST

- ☐ Your business blueprint reflects the optimal way to think about your business and how your products/service lines create and deliver value.

- ☐ You have developed and cascaded OKRs throughout your functions and main departments, creating cohesive, strategic golden threads through the business. Your key results are SMART and backed up by good strategic plans.

- ☐ Knowing which needles are important to move, your business heatmap reflects where the business needs to focus attention, time, and money across management, people, processes, and technology.

- ☐ You are aligning and driving your people around deliberate values and behaviors (in turn, creating a culture) that will foster a high-performing team that achieves OKRs.

- ☐ You have a granular leadership heatmap, and you know the big changes and investments needed to ensure the team gets the right direction, guidance, and role modeling from the top.

CHAPTER 5
IMPROVE

"Change is easy to propose,
hard to implement, and
especially hard to sustain."

—ANDY HARGREAVES

You have now done the strategic diagnostic groundwork required. Welcome to probably the most valuable, and least understood, sphere of the SHIFT™ Business Operating System: "Improve."

Freeing a Founder is a step change. There are probably a handful of other step changes that you can make in your business—including implementing SHIFT™ processes and structures—that will unlock significant, self-sustaining value and growth.

Remember, you explicitly captured your shortlist of desired achievements in your objectives and key results (OKRs) in the previous chapter. Now, you need to consider *how* you achieve those and what improvements you can make in the business to enable that performance.

> **YOUR KEY RESULTS ARE WHAT YOU NEED TO ACHIEVE. "IMPROVE" IS THE SPHERE THAT WILL HELP YOUR LINE MANAGERS FIGURE OUT HOW TO ACHIEVE IT!**

There are changes that need to be made, and your managers have a business to run. They can't focus time on people, process, customers, cross-functional problem solving, *and* strategic projects. Taking strategic projects seriously—doubling down on identifying them, driving them, and making them stick—will unlock untold potential and resilience in your business.

So, while this is going to seem alien to most small to medium-sized businesses, it's probably the most valuable alien you can embrace. With that in mind, let me give you a tour of "Improve."

There are three core components here:

1. **Business process optimization:** Understand what your core processes are, map them out, and assess how to optimize them.

2. **Top 3 | 10 Hitlist:** Identify and prioritize which strategic projects you need to double down on to achieve your OKRs.

3. **Change resourcing:** Make sure you resource the above very effectively (in other words, *do not* rely solely on your line managers).

BUSINESS PROCESS OPTIMIZATION

Growth comes from efficiency and scalability of value-adding processes (including your demand-generating processes like marketing). Very few businesses that I have worked with actually know how their processes work, what "good" looks like, or where the real bottlenecks and opportunities lie. Using your strategy (value drivers) and harmony (OKRs), you can isolate what the heart of the business is—including the associated veins and arteries—and make sure that system is singing.

This is business process optimization (BPO).

Now, before you start thinking about Visio diagrams and diamonds and boxes, this is *strategic* business process mapping. Everything you are doing is 80/20! You take a top-down, 80/20 view on which processes and which *parts* of those processes you should look to optimize. You don't go "Visio mad." In fact, you won't even use Visio. For the purposes of identifying the big needle-moving opportunities, you focus more on the bigger process chunks and the associated bigger opportunities.

A solid approach to business process optimization will unlock the highest value for the business, and make sure the changes happen quickly and effectively.

Identifying big improvement opportunities is driven from both the top down—via OKRs, as well as known bottlenecks and issues—and bottom up, by identifying improvement opportunities through short and sharp diagnostics of priority business processes.

I'm going to touch on a few useful BPO concepts so you can see how practical and powerful they can be. They are: the diagnostic process; brown paper exercises; DILO (day in the life of); and ideal diary.

How these are used, to what extent, and with what tools is very business- and situation-dependent. The focus should always be on 80/20 impact and effectiveness.

A DIAGNOSTIC PROCESS USES VARIOUS BPO TOOLS TO MAP OUT HOW A CORE PROCESS WORKS AND DOES A TOP-DOWN ASSESSMENT OF IMPROVEMENT OPPORTUNITIES.

You start with a strategic analysis (OKRs, value driver trees, and so on) to understand the playing field. You then conduct idea generation and lever analysis. I suggest doing these together so you can run targeted idea-generation workshops on specific hotspots. Once ideas are assessed and prioritized, they are roadmapped, work-planned, and implemented. This may be done as part of the strategic projects funnel, unless the whole diagnostic process is a strategic project that has already passed through the funnel.

These exercises are *extremely* collaborative. They use as much of the team as possible to both understand what really happens, and to tap into everyone's improvement ideas. Linking back to culture, this is a very hands-on way of getting the team involved in shaping the new "grown-up" business and being a core part of the journey.

BPO diagnostics

Thorough diagnostics are a rigorous way to analyze your core processes—identifying inefficiencies and improvement opportunities, and codifying the most optimal way of doing things (for training and performance management). While these diagnostics can be done at gross levels of detail, for our Founder-freeing purposes we would target your most important processes and take a very 80/20 approach to identify high-impact quick wins. Here's a template you can work off of:

	TOP-DOWN STRATEGIC ANALYSIS	BOTTOM-UP IDEA GENERATION & LEVER ANALYSIS	WORKPLANNING & ROADMAP	PROGRAM MANAGEMENT
OUTPUTS	• Strategic operational heatmap • Estimated size-of-the-prize across key processes / departments • Hypothesis trees	• Baseline understanding of core processes and core-process performance • Waste and opportunity analyses across core processes • Prioritized improvement programs with back-of-the-envelope value estimates and ease-of-capture assessments	• Program repository, pareto and opportunity build up • Prioritised Program Roadmap with owner and stakeholder mapping • Resourcing optimization	• Macro program tracker • Program dashboards • Workstream post-mortems • Improvement organization heatmap • Line led change and adoption
ACTIVITIES	• Strategic review of performance gaps in light of business strategy • Define key targets and aspirations	• Collaboratively process map core processes • Analyse waste and opportunities for improvement • Identify improvement opportunities – think "Program" rather than "idea" • Prioritize programs of work in line with OKRs and Strategy	• Improvement Roadmap compiled to balance priority value capture with change capacity (Optimization Steering Committee) • Key initiative one pagers detailing opportunity synthesis	• Program Management Office / Program Manager assigned • Improvement MOS designed and dovetailed into business MOS • Steerco and Escalation mechanisms defined
TOOLS	• Strategic Financial Model and value driver tree • Founder Heatmap • OKRs	• Deep structured interviews • Brown paper business process mapping with artifact and RACI analyses • Idea generation sessions leveraging Strategic Prioritization Framework • Activity value add analyses, DILOs and Ideal Diary deviance	• Priority Program business cases (80/20) • Key Program Gantts • Resource allocation and prioritization	• Progress tracking • Process debottlenecking • Medium Term Planning and pre-emptive wheel greasing • Agile program management

Brown paper exercises

A key part of diagnostics and general business process optimization is a "brown paper exercise." This is effectively interactive process mapping, traditionally done on a large wall covered in brown paper. Post-it notes, markers, printouts, and so forth end up plastered all over the wall as the actual process is mapped out in detail. With geographically spread teams, it is sometimes useful to use online whiteboard tools such as Miro so that the broader team can weigh in.

Effective brown paper exercises are best facilitated by someone who is not familiar with the process being mapped—this avoids assumptions being made, steps being overlooked, or shortcuts being taken.

DILO

"Day in the life of" analysis is just that—analyzing what someone does in a day to get a good sense of the real work, what gets in the way, and practical impediments to "theoretically perfect." Here's a slightly off-kilter, albeit real-world example:

> I ran a DILO in a gym once, following a pair of maintenance officers around for a couple of days. It was as invasive and uncomfortable as it sounds, but it was invaluable.

> One gym business had bought another gym business, and there was an opportunity to have one maintenance team working across several gyms of different brands, all of which had been brought into the same stable. We figured we would do a proper BPO analysis while we were at it.

> This is how I found myself, notebook in hand, in the men's changeroom, watching this poor maintenance guy alternate between fighting with the sauna steam system, fixing broken lockers, and painting over scuff marks on walls.

Obviously, people work harder when they are being watched/stalked. Despite that, I identified a ton of practical opportunities to make the whole maintenance process more efficient—to the tune of a 50% reduction in time required—with some really simple decisions and tools.

Once you've worked to eliminate waste from the different tasks and processes people do, and optimized the remaining work, you then define what an ideal day or week looks like. This leads us to:

Ideal diary

While you are assessing and defining the "people" part of processes, it is often beneficial to create an ideal diary. This is a deliberate view of how much time someone in a particular role should be spending on what, on a daily, weekly, or monthly basis.

The concept behind an ideal diary is simple: What would a perfect day, week, or month look like in the calendar of a particular role?

THIS IS ABOUT DETERMINING HOW PEOPLE SHOULD BE EXPECTED TO SPEND THEIR TIME, AND ASSESSING HOW MUCH CAPACITY A PARTICULAR ROLE REASONABLY HAS.

I have used this prolifically in my own businesses to understand what is possible, and to give people clear guidance on how to spend their time. And you shouldn't take a purely theoretical view of this: you need to account for reasonable distractions, surprises, and "just shooting the shit" with colleagues. Denying these realities would be silly.

I have used this with all my new people leaders and executives, to give us an aligned view of where their time should be invested. I've used this for sales administrators, quality assurance staff, gym maintenance staff—you can apply this thinking to any role to help structure an individual's work and focus. I've included a senior manager example below.

Once I have the week structured at a macro level, I can then put meetings in their desired bucket. As seen in the example, managers and project leaders know to schedule any project meetings on a Wednesday as that is the day dedicated to project meetings. Managers and others with direct reports know that Tuesday is the day for BAU meetings.

MON	TUE	WED	THUR	FRI
Exec check-ins and planning sessions	Weekly / fortnightly ops reviews and planning sessions	Project steercos and functional strategy sessions	Support function reviews, planning and strategy	Board / shareholders
				R&D
LUNCH / BUFFER				
Ad hoc meetings / working time	Weekly / fortnightly ops reviews and planning sessions	Ad hoc meetings / working time	Exec one-on-ones	Ad hoc meetings / working time
			6 weekly coaching one-on-ones	

Give a new manager a pie chart of how they should be spending their time—like how many hours per week they should be spending on one-on-ones versus projects versus department meetings, for example—and they will be eternally grateful that they don't need to read your mind to know what your expectations are! After all, time is the key currency of management.

Proactively giving any staff member clear guidelines on how they should divide up their time is equally valuable.

As mentioned, these are only a handful of useful business process optimization tools that I have routinely used. A seasoned BPO specialist would know these well, plus a wealth of other methodologies and tools.

The outcome? A very deep and thorough understanding of the core business processes, a comprehensive view of the waste and opportunities in the system, and a prioritized list of strategic projects and other initiatives that can put the process on steroids.

These strategic projects will form a subset of:

TOP 3 | 10 HITLIST

To best facilitate a Founder's exit—and ensure the remaining management team has a clear, prioritized list of improvements they are expected to focus on—you need a strategic project hitlist. That's a prioritized *hitlist*, not a wish list!

I call this the Top 3 | 10 Hitlist.

What is your list of ten programs or projects that are going to significantly move the needle in the next twelve months? And of those ten, which are the three that you simply *must* kick off and get implemented ASAP?

Strategic projects are the big, bold, needle-moving programs that are going to smash your key results. These are such things as hiring a GM, restructuring functions, performance management programs, full operational process transformations, or implementing a tech solution to "go paperless."

Some strategic projects require project management, business analytics, business process optimization, identifying and managing trade-offs, investments, piloting, training, communications, and change management.

Strategic projects, by definition, have your strategy and your OKRs at heart. Everything that you think about changing in the business, in a big way, has to unlock business value, and have your objectives and key results at its core.

If there is any program or major initiative in your funnel or roadmap that doesn't explicitly link to achieving a key result, it is distracting you from your key results!

By their very nature, strategic projects are 80/20.

WHAT ARE THE BIG, BOLD CHANGES THE BUSINESS CAN MAKE (WITH YOU, THE FOUNDER) TO "FREE THE FOUNDER" AND DRIVE BUSINESS GROWTH GOING FORWARD?

It is the embodiment of strategic problem solving and projects that will really move the needle.

When thinking about strategic programs and projects, they may be solution- and key result–oriented ("We need to make the contracts department paperless"), or they may be problem-focused ("Imports are often two weeks late from supplier X, and this is pissing off our customers—we need someone to work with supplier X to fix this!").

YOU SIMPLY DON'T HAVE THE TIME OR TOLERANCE FOR CHANGE THAT IS HELPFUL BUT NOT VALUABLE.

Time, attention, and focus are limited resources. Every minute spent on changing or improving something that doesn't move the needle is a minute getting in the way of actually moving the needle. Stop doing it, stop resourcing it. Threaten to fire anyone who talks about it.

THE WORD "NO" IS A CRITICAL STRATEGIC IMPROVEMENT TOOL.

Top 3 | 10 Roadmap

The Top 3 | 10 Hitlist is then transformed into a Top 3 | 10 Roadmap—a centralized Gantt chart of the strategic projects you are running in the business.

This roadmap allows you to set expectations, manage resources, define milestones, assign accountability, and track progress. Without this and associated project governance (coming up in Chapter 6), projects get started and never get finished. You simply do not have time for that. It's wasteful, creates distractions, and impacts culture really badly, as the following example highlights.

HAVING AND MANAGING A STRATEGIC PROJECTS ROADMAP SUCCESSFULLY IS THE BRIDGE BETWEEN YOUR BOARDROOM STRATEGY AND FRONTLINE PERFORMANCE.

I was sitting in an OKR-setting session with a continuous improvement department. The GM, Mike, started by going through the strategy and the strategic narrative. He succinctly but comprehensively unpacked the challenges of the last two years, what customers needed, and what operational performance improvements were mission-critical to focus on over the coming twelve months. Mike called out one production line in particular that was a huge strategic hotspot. Throughput was currently operating at 25% below benchmark.

While Mike was explaining this, one of the CI manager's faces caught my attention. With every passing word, his jaw dropped lower and lower, and his eyes got bigger and bigger.

When the GM finished with the strategic context setting, he asked if there were any questions. I said I had one. I turned to the CI manager, Joel, and said, "I've been watching your reactions to Mike's points, and I'm interested to know what's going through your mind."

Joel responded, "You know that critical operational area Mike is so worried about? We have been doing so much work in that space over the last year. But none of it has been focused on improving throughput. We've spent endless hours with that management team. And I've just realized that every hour we have spent with that team is an hour that they weren't focused on improving throughput!"

If we had a centralized view of all the changes happening in the business, we would have spotted that problem ages ago!

A Top 3 | 10 Roadmap is not an MS Project file with one million line items in it. It's a one-pager containing the macro plans for your Top 3 | 10 Hitlist, which everyone can see on a projector screen. Here's an example:

Activity	Mar	Apr	May	Jun	Jul	Aug	Sep	Oct	Nov	Dec	Responsible
Strategy: Mission											Tom
Sign off annual strategy											
Agree Exco process, OKRs											
Cascade OKRs											
Values redefinition											
Budget update											Vicky
Revise budget and capital strategy											
Performance Management Program											Simone
Target setting analytics											
Team lead training and roll out											
MOS review to incorporate											
Leadership Development Program											Simone
Sign off organogram											
Recruit for leadership vacancies											
Design program and design / source content											
Roll out program with new team											
Insurance Product Launch											Nick
Insurance Product Design and Pricing											
GTM Strategy											
Pilot											
Training and ops handover											
CRM System upgrade											Amit
Scoping and POCs											
Business spec and platform decision											
Wave 1 implementation											
Wave 2 implementation											
Helpdesk Insourcing											Amit
Migrate to new helpdesk system											
Establish team and function											
Helpdesk Training											
Helpdesk Review and CI											
Internal Process Improvement											Maria
Customer Success Brown Paper & BPO											
Agile Dev BPO											Duncan

If this is well-categorized and -administered, it allows you to assess and plan:

- How long a project should take
- Who is doing it and how much time is required
- Any change or technical resources needed
- Change investment and timing
- Operations disruptions and change load (don't change two systems or processes in the same fortnight)
- Project management of progress and dependencies
- Your strategic pipeline in value

Setting up your roadmap allows you to see what opportunities there are, what the business cases for those opportunities are, and how much you may want to invest in expediting the roadmap.

Once set, your roadmap is reviewed monthly, and any new ideas or priorities are weighed up and planned in the roadmap. The roadmap then becomes your central source of truth. Project plans, statuses, and documentation are all kept up to date in your roadmap platform for central management and access.

Thereafter, any surprises, disruptions, or urgent changes in the business that may affect the roadmap can be structurally addressed. This would include changing the timing of projects and milestones, reassigning resources, or even eliminating projects to make space.

Once the Top 3 | 10 Roadmap is in place, it *codifies your thinking* about how to prioritize work and investment. This systematizes how you think about making big changes in the business, and how to trade off options and investments.

Obviously, you will weigh in on material strategic changes in the business as a "free" Founder and Board member. However, through this process you are teaching your management team how to prioritize like you do. And now, finally, you have a structure to do that with.

CHANGE RESOURCING

So, who is going to deliver your Top 3? These initiatives simply *must* get done, and must get done quickly and successfully!

STRATEGIC PROJECTS ARE NOT THE JOB OF YOUR MANAGEMENT TEAM!

If your managers are 80/20 thinkers, enjoy running business process optimization projects, and are hypothesis-driven operators, they are probably crap managers and should be running strategic projects!

Your managers' jobs are to be 80/20 *people and process managers*. They are built to manage people, worry about day-to-day processes, and fight fires. Yes, they are meant to *implement* and own change, sure. But they simply do not have enough time, focus, or, frankly, skills to properly drive strategic change in the business.

Strategic-projects rock stars are highly analytical, love working on projects, and are influential but don't like managing frontline ops people. Here are some examples:

In my first business, I quickly hired a single strategic projects person, an ex-McKinsey consultant, who was given a new product launch to look after. Project management, problem solving, prototyping, proof of concept, pricing strategy—you name it. My managers were too busy running the business and didn't have the time or the skills to incubate and then launch a whole new product.

By the time we were around 400 staff strong, we had a projects team of ten business analysts, led by an ex-McKinsey engagement manager. They were each assigned to a strategic project (working next to a line owner/champion) and were responsible for end-to-end project management, business analytics, process optimization, stakeholder management, data analytics, steerco management, systems testing coordination, and so on.

My initial strategic projects hire eventually became the CTO for the business.

Another of our projects people was a math guru:

> *Adam was one of our project associates—what a weapon. A master's degree in mathematics, and in a "boy band." He liked chess, math, and girls. We were scaling a direct-to-consumer life insurance business. Each day we ran hundreds of marketing ads, and at any given time were managing 20,000 sales leads. These all went into a CRM system that fed our (growing) sales call center. Adam led a project to determine how to prioritize these leads with a dynamic scoring algorithm. The math was a small part of the job—working with the executive to determine the right priorities, flexing the scoring algorithm and checking that leads didn't get "stuck" being deprioritized, and monitoring downstream feedback on quality and conversion rates. This was a big cross-functional project that unlocked massive value for the business.*

In my second startup, we hired a misfit/renegade named Nicole:

> *I used to skydive a lot. One Saturday evening at the drop zone, I noticed a young woman sitting at the bar by herself. The skydiving community is a small one, and a lonely, single visitor to the drop zone after dark is pretty unusual. I went over to introduce myself, to make friends and include this visitor in our weird community.*

> *Her name was Nicole, and she had just moved out of the city and was having a quarter-life crisis. We had a long chat (as I'd had many quarter-life crises before), and we swapped notes. We became friends. It wasn't long before Nicole got involved in running operations at the drop zone—organizing who was on which skydiving run, and looking after the pilots. Eventually, Nicole was leading the coordination of national skydiving competitions and cross-border events. Nicole was great. She was always smiling, partied with us at night but was up at the crack of dawn, and ran a smooth operation. And running a smooth operation with a bunch of skydivers is no easy feat!*

Parallel to all of this, I was in the middle of co-founding a new tech startup. Things had taken shape, and we were looking to bring on our first employee. I knew exactly who that should be. I gave Nicole a call, and asked her if it was time to leave the countryside once more and come back to building a career. The answer was a resounding "Yes!"

Nicole was employee number one, and her first day was spent sitting side by side with me and my fellow co-founders in an airline lounge that doubled as our office.

Shortly after, we secured a small office space and had our shareholders around to see the sites and have a board meeting. We discussed our progress, and they inquired about the background and profile of our first employee. I commented, "Nicole is great. A real go-getter. She will roll up her sleeves and do whatever we need."

We walked back to the office, through the door, and found Nicole on hands and knees, vacuuming under the desks. "I just couldn't take it anymore!" she exclaimed.

Fast forward seven years, and Nicole has worked her way from customer service consultant, to financial advisor, to training manager, to project manager, to executive of projects, IT and BI!

Nicole was a misfit. A renegade. A go-getter and executor with a great analytical mind.

These aren't project managers. These are executors and optimizers—they roll up their sleeves and make change happen. And any good business process optimizer is smart enough to manage a strategic project. You need a handful of these, and you need to keep them busy.

You probably have a Nicole hiding out somewhere in your business. Find her, train her, and then let her loose! If you don't have this kind of profile in your business, you may need to consider getting a consultant in for a couple of months to help rapidly drive and scale your strategic change initiatives.

Either way, find someone who is familiar with this stuff and can do it in their sleep. Bring them in to help you apply it to your business, while you just focus on the results. The ROI is a no-brainer!

Remember, freeing the Founder (you) is one step change that will cascade many other healthy and value-adding changes in the business. You are now set up for improvement success. While you drive and embed your "Improve" sphere, operations managers will **FOCUS** on the delivery of their OKRs.

IMPROVE TO-DO LIST

☐ You have deliberately primed, rallied, and excited the team around the changes and rapid evolution you are about to trigger. You are marrying internal comms, change management, and role modeling to foster conviction and excitement in the team.

☐ You clearly understand the core value-driving processes and systems in the business. You have thoroughly diagnosed the opportunities and issues within these processes, applying solid business process management techniques.

☐ You have identified your Top 3 | 10 Hitlist of strategic projects that will support your OKRs, and addressed priority issues and opportunities within your core business process.

☐ Your Top 3 | 10 Roadmap will guide implementation, prioritization, and change load in the business. Proactively managing your Top 3 | 10 strategic projects will ensure blockers are eliminated and delivery is ensured and accelerated.

☐ You have carefully considered change resourcing to ensure your operations management are not overwhelmed with project work and can still effectively run the business while changing the business.

CHAPTER 6
FOCUS

*"Strategy is a pattern in
a stream of decisions."*

– HENRY MINTZBERG

S o, you've articulated your ongoing strategy and set a compelling mission for your leadership team to embark on. You have harmonized your structures, responsibilities, and skills to effectively drive OKRs. You have consolidated and focused your improvement efforts to optimize *how* you operate in key business areas so you can free yourself as the Founder.

Now, the business needs to run and achieve its key results with focus. Planning. Delivering. Problem solving. Unblocking.

Continuously improving. Growing. Achieving.

Behaviors at all levels and across all functions can be reinforced and encouraged with real focus, just as they can also be vaporized and thrown into disarray with poor focus.

Real focus comes from the way the leadership team maintains its strategic course—keeping everyone on track and everyone's eyes on their respective prizes without you, the Founder, running around and being the business operating system. This is done through:

- your business performance dashboard,
- your management operating system (MOS),
- effective meetings, and
- effective communication skills and solid strategic problem solving.

YOUR BUSINESS PERFORMANCE DASHBOARD

Returning to our orchestra analogy, the conductor is an important part of the orchestra and symphony. The conductor has a "balcony view" of what is happening, the tempo of the musicians, and the relative volume.

In a Founder-led business, this is most often the role of the Founder. But what if the orchestra could self-regulate? Couldn't you use a dashboard of measures and metrics so that the first violinist can see that they are too loud, and adjust accordingly?

This is your business performance dashboard.

"You can't manage what you can't measure" is a quote attributed to business management expert Peter Drucker. And we often hear the converse: you manage what you measure.

Having a clear and transparent overview of business performance is critical to your business operating system. This is not a P&L—this is an overview of the core value drivers of the business, measured and monitored at the right level of granularity to drive decision making and proactive management.

Coming out of your value driver analysis in "Strategy," your OKRs in "Harmony," and the key metrics you want to move in "Improve," you have a good understanding of the headline metrics you care about, both across the business and for each main function.

Your business performance dashboard collates all of these into a central, shared source of truth and synthesis of how the business is tracking relative to targets. Here's an example:

BUSINESS PERFORMANCE DASHBOARD

USD

METRIC	SOURCE	OWNER	TYPE	W1	W2	W3	W4	W5	MONTH	TARGET	STATUS	COMMENTARY
CORE PERFORMANCE METRICS												
REVENUE (INVOICED)	Xero	Tom	Total	436 892	393 421	408 121	635 279	196 261	2 069 973	1 755 000	EXCEEDING	
REVENUE PER EMPLOYEE	Calc		Ave	1 259	1 134	1 176	1 831	566	5 965	5 014	EXCEEDING	
CASH IN (RECEIVED)	Bank feed		Total	428 154	385 553	412 406	628 926	192 336	2 047 374	2 069 973	OKAY	
# OF SALES	Salesforce	Tom	Total	565	518	542	769	243	2 637	2 340	EXCEEDING	
AVE REVENUE PER SALE	Calc	Tom	Ave	773	760	753	826	808	785	750	EXCEEDING	
AVE COST OF CUSTOMER ACQUISITION	Calc	Maria	Ave	193	201	188	165	167	183	214	EXCEEDING	
MARKETING												
AVE COST OF CUSTOMER ACQUISITION	Calc	Maria	Ave	193	201	188	165	167	183	214	CAUTION	
DIRECT MARKETING SPEND		Maria	Total	109 223	104 118	101 896	126 885	40 581	482 703	500 000	EXCEEDING	Deploy more spend!
# LEADS		Maria	Total	6 647	5 886	5 531	7 539	2 209	27 812	26 000	EXCEEDING	
# QUALIFIED LEADS TO SALES		Maria	Total	2 792	2 413	2 046	3 468	950	11 669	11 700	OKAY	
LEAD TO TRANSFER RATIO		Maria	%	42%	41%	37%	46%	43%	43%	45%	CAUTION	
AVE COST PER LEAD		Maria	Ave	16	18	18	17	18	17	19	CAUTION	Ensure increased spend and volume do
CONVERSION RATIO	Calc	Maria / Tom	%	8.5%	8.8%	9.8%	10.2%	11.0%	9.5%	9.0%	OKAY	
SALES												
REVENUE		Tom	Total	436 892	393 421	408 121	635 279	196 261	2 069 973	1 755 000	EXCEEDING	
# OF SALES		Tom	Total	565	518	542	769	243	2 637	2 340	EXCEEDING	
AVE REVENUE PER SALE	Calc	Tom	Ave	773	760	753	826	808	785	750	EXCEEDING	
# PRE QUALIFIED LEADS	Calc	Maria	Total	2 792	2 413	2 046	3 468	960	11 669	11 700	OKAY	
QUOTE RATIO	Calc	Tom	%	73%	77%	71%	79%	77%	76%	70%	EXCEEDING	
CONVERSION RATIO	Calc	Maria / Tom	%	8.5%	8.8%	9.8%	10.2%	11.0%	9.5%	9%	OKAY	
CUSTOMER SUPPORT												

A few key notes and learnings:

- Do not automate this. You want your team to engage with the numbers, understand the numbers, and *synthesize* the insights that the numbers are giving them.

- The dashboard should include your headline value drivers—both leading and lagging. Some metrics tell you what has happened (sales), and some give you an indication of what may happen (number of client proposals sent and average conversion rates).

- It must be shared. All senior managers should share one dashboard. This drives transparency and accountability.

- It must include synthesized commentary on what is happening with the metric and actions to be taken. Your dashboard is not a report. It is not data. It is a *management tool*. Anyone looking at the dashboard should be able to see the status of a metric, *why* it is that status, and what is being done about lagging performance metrics.

- Metrics must be measured at a frequency relevant for proactive management and intervention. In some high-volume businesses (call-center sales, for instance), daily figures may be relevant to tweak and change marketing, especially if you're running thousands of digital marketing ads a day. For B2B SaaS with big-ticket enterprise contracts, daily activity is noisy and not worth tracking. Apply your mind to your business and management, and determine what the right granularity of time tracking should be. If in doubt, start with weekly tracking.

The dashboard will guide and support the management team members' commentary on their respective monthly performance review synthesis (more on this soon). Your dashboard will also be a key ingredient in your management operating system, which we'll look at in the next section.

In the short to medium term, I always look to implement weekly or fortnightly senior management standups (thirty minutes long) around the business performance dashboard. This drives implementation and accountability, shifting the team into proactive problem solving to get ahead of the metrics and make change happen faster.

One of the bigger challenges Founder-led management teams face is that managers tend to stay in their lane. With the Founder (you) around to be the sounding board, director, and decision maker, there isn't any incentive or need for managers to direct or weigh in outside of their sphere of direct influence. In order to free yourself as the Founder, you need to leverage group accountability and peer coaching/thought leadership as much as possible.

Using your business performance dashboard and weekly or fortnightly standups, you can get the team to *answer to each other* and cross-collaborate, with you, the Founder, as facilitator.

While this would be a key addition to the diaries of many Founder-led businesses, it's important to look at the entire management operating system, holistically, to cover all horizons in the context of management responsibilities.

YOUR MANAGEMENT OPERATING SYSTEM

You wouldn't be blamed for thinking that a management operating system (MOS) is "just the meetings we have." This is a common misconception of a poorly thought-through MOS.

> **YOUR MOS DEFINES HOW MANAGERS SHARE INFORMATION AND MAKE DECISIONS TO ACHIEVE YOUR KEY RESULTS.**

In contrast, a well-thought-out MOS defines how information is cascaded and reported, as well as how to plan, review progress, set priorities, problem solve, escalate, collaborate, stay on course, and change course. The basis of the MOS is information flows and collaboration to *make decisions* in order to achieve key results.

Before we go any further, I would like to put a controversial statement on the table:

THE FUNDAMENTAL JOB OF A SENIOR MANAGER IS TO BE IN MEETINGS.

There. I said it. And I *firmly* believe it.

Managers are paid to manage. To coordinate. To steer. In a well-oiled organizational system, managers react to information, problem solve, make decisions, and mobilize resources. This means that individual contributors should be bringing information and proposals to meetings with managers for them to weigh in on.

The only individual contribution managers should be making is executive reporting and escalations. The rest of the time, managers should be meeting with people—with a focus on problem solving, facilitating collaboration, and helping them deliver their key results and develop as people!

The management team needs to juggle different objectives and key results at different levels of abstraction. Often, these get crossed.

When you are discussing strategy, mission, and business objectives, you are actively engaging in abstract reasoning. You are imagining possibilities and looking outward. You consider scenarios and join abstract dots to bring conclusions back to now.

This is very different from how your brain engages in analytical reasoning on monthly progress to deliver departmental key results. Breaking down tangible relationships and processes, identifying bottlenecks, analyzing where responsibilities lie—this is very tangible critical thinking. And, in my experience, you don't change gears very quickly.

To drive the right focus in the business, managers must be able to do their "deep work" at a:

- Strategic level (strategy, value propositions, competitive advantage, long-term org changes, functional strategies, competitor reviews)

- Tactical running level (KPIs, postmortems, budgets, targets, highs, lows)

- Tactical changing level (project meetings, operational problem solving and innovation, how to change the machine)

A MOS has these deliberate planning horizons. For a typical function and department, there are four horizons:

- **Annual strategy and budget reviews**—drive the five-year plan

- **Quarterly strategic reviews**—drive the one-year plan

- **Monthly performance reviews** and **priority setting around key results**—drive the quarterly plan

- **Weekly or fortnightly operations reviews** and **priority setting around KPIs and KPAs**—drive the monthly plan

The team needs to be deliberate about having *different* meetings to ensure they are properly covering objectives, key results, and shorter-term underlying KPIs across the different layers of the business and planning horizons. This is where things can get horribly lost in the weeds, and where "death by meetings" can occur.

Some things can be shared via dashboards, some via email in narrative or qualitative form. Some things need to be talked about. Some don't.

	Weekly	Monthly	Quarterly	Yearly
Strategy	Weekly / Fortnightly Senior Management Standup	Monthly Exec meeting	Quarterly Business Strategic Reviews	Annual Business Performance, Strategy and Budget Review
Change	Sprint reviews Project standups	Monthly Improve Steerco Project problem solving	Quarterly Improve Strategic Reviews Project wrap-up reviews	Annual Improve Performance, Strategy and Budget review
Delivery	Weekly team meetings Standups	Monthly department meeting Monthly 1:1s	Quarterly Functional Strategic Review	Semi-annual staff Performance Reviews — Annual Ops Performance, Strategy and Budget Review
	Weekly Drive delivery of monthly targets	**Monthly** Drive delivery of quarterly KRs	**Quarterly** Drive delivery of annual Objectives	**Yearly** Drive 5-year Strategy

THE CORE OF THE MOS IS WEEK-TO-WEEK AND MONTH-TO-MONTH PLANNING. THE KEY QUESTION IS: "WHAT DO WE NEED TO DECIDE AND DO DIFFERENTLY TO ACHIEVE OR ACCELERATE OUR KEY RESULTS?"

A useful exercise in this respect is to run a collaborative MOS design process with the management team and people leaders. Below is an example output from one of my sessions. Don't worry—you're not supposed to be able to read the details. Along the left-hand side and the top are the various functions we were concerned with. The brief was:

- Left to right: I am Function x, and I need to share this information with Function n.

- Top to bottom: I am Function x, and I need to get this information from Function n.

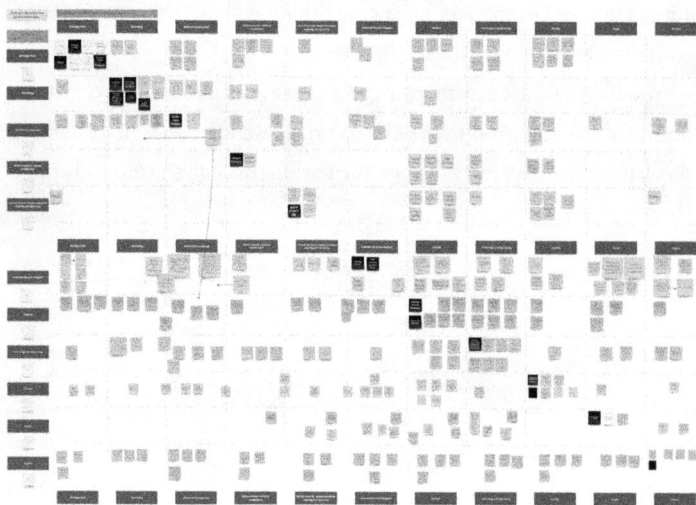

How doesn't feature yet. This was just a comprehensive view of all the information, insights, so-whats, and forward and backward thinking that needed to be shared in order to know what was going on, and to *make sure plans to achieve key results talk to one another.*

Workshopping this was great as it gave an insightful and holistic view, and allowed managers to explain to the broader group why certain information was important to them to perform their function. There were some interesting insights along the way.

Turning all this into a set of engagements is an art. Below are some points to keep in mind, as well as some examples:

Firstly, whatever can be housed on a self-service dashboard for information sharing should be there. However, you shouldn't assume the team will look at it and engage properly.

Secondly, map out the major engagements the team needs, each with its unique purpose. Then, do an audience analysis to check for duplication or severe overlap (while thinking about the levels of management abstraction).

You then package meetings and plot them (and all other major responsibilities like one-on-one meetings) on a calendar view. This helps to check the chronological flow of information through the monthly cycle.

MOS H1

	Tom	Natalie	Sandra	Bill	Isaac	Janet	Mary	Talia	Reg A leads	Reg B leads	Reg C leads	HR	Comms	IT	xxx	xxx
Monthly Business Review (2hrs)	✓	✓	✓	✓	✓	✓	✓	✓				✓	✓			
Monthly People check in (1hr)	✓	✓	✓	✓	✓	✓	✓	✓								
Monthly Strategic Projects Steerco	✓		Opt	✓	✓	✓	✓	✓					✓			
Monthly Technology Steerco	Opt	Opt	Opt		✓	✓	✓	✓						✓		
Region A monthly performance review	✓		✓						✓							
Monthly A P1 performance review	✓		✓				✓		✓							
Monthly A P2 performance review	✓		✓				✓		✓							
Region A Qrt Strategic Review	✓		✓						✓			✓				
Region B monthly performance review		✓								✓						
Monthly B P1 & 2 performance review		✓					✓			✓						
Two-Monthly B P3 performance review		✓					✓			✓						
Reg. B Qrt Strategic Review										✓		✓				
Reg C monthly performance review	✓										✓	✓				
Monthly Reg C 1:1s	✓						✓				✓					
Reg C Qrt Strategic Review	✓										✓	✓				

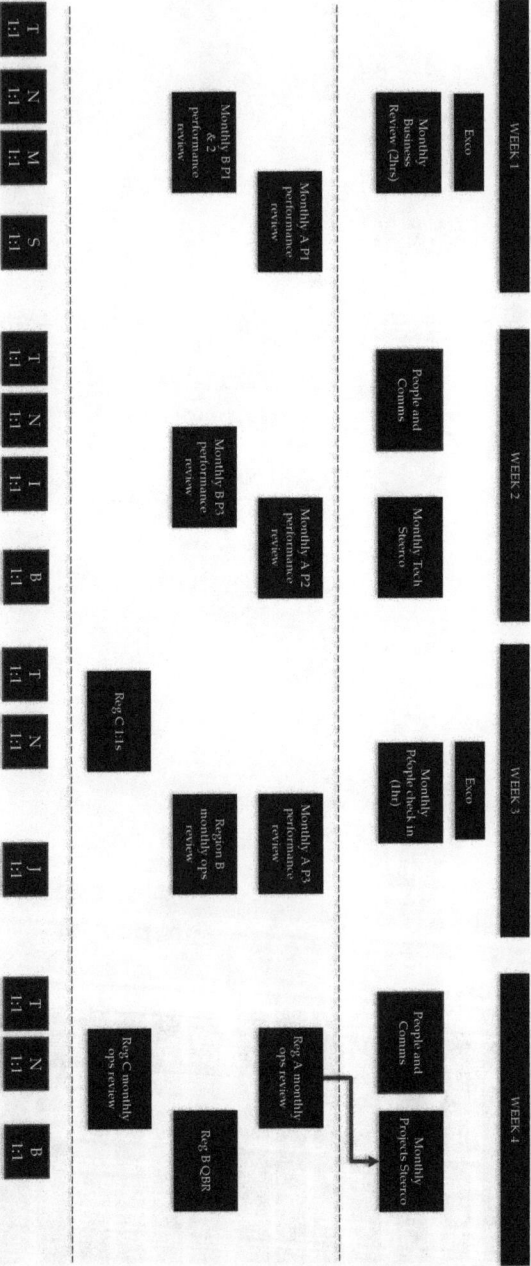

Note: you will not get this right the first time, and the maturity of the discussions, information, and overall MOS will evolve during SHIFT™ implementation. It is good to give it a go for three months and then adjust. Cancel meetings. Collapse meetings. Shorten meetings. Whatever. Have a deliberate review with learnings, and refine the MOS to make sure the right key result topics are discussed with the right people at the right frequency.

Now, what do you talk about in your meetings? You have focused your meetings around a discrete set of "purposes," and you need to have good key result–based discussions with the people in the room to drive accountability. The key word here is "synthesis"! It is critical to drive focus, insights, and discussions by avoiding lengthy slide decks and documents. I use two key pieces of paper:

1. **Monthly performance review synthesis template.** Here, you want a maximum of three to five bullet points in each block. The focus for each should be highlights and priorities—not everything going on!

Monthly Performance Review Synthesis

2. **OKR dashboard**. This is a one-pager with the relevant OKRs, accompanied by a Harvey ball status update and a field for "Action." For any under-threat or lagging OKR, you need to see a remedial action, escalation, or cross-functional "help needed" to unblock the key result and drive progress.

H2 2024 Customer Success OKRs

○ Critical issues. Exec escalation required   ◑ Material issues. Snr Mgr escalations required   ◐ Lagging. Remedial actions known and planned   ◐ KR tracking positive   ● KR attainment secure

Owner & Accountability: TOM

Deliver best in class customer success outcomes through high performance operations

- KR: Achieving >96% three-month adoption rates by December ◑
- KR: Delivering at a unit cost average of $20k per project unit ◐
  - Action: Project process diagnostic underway; Admin outsourcing to low-cost centre POC ongoing
- KR: Moving NPS scores from 55 to 75 by December ●
- KR: Unlocking technology quick wins (low investment changes) to support efficiency and consistency – unlocking $20m internal cost savings by June ◐
  - Action: Implementation of Jira delayed by a month but on track with revised project plan

Deliver our distinctive new Product X to market

- KR: Build a bench of 20 customer success specialists across Europe to support GTM by June. ●
- KR: Deliver 50 Product X projects by December with average NPS of 70. ◑
  - Action: Reliant on admin outsourcing above or may have FTE bottlenecks
- KR: Drive Product X adoption of 90% and generate cross sell opportunities of $20m for Q1 ◐
  - Action: Product X adoption KSFs still hypothetical. Focus on this in Q3 and Q4 and build into project plans to frontload

Operate with a strong performance culture

- KR: Support the implementation of our broad-based culture and fun strategy by Aug ●
- KR: Identify consistent top performers by end July – codify performance best practices in training material by end Aug ◐
- KR: Implement performance management infrastructure, Project Manager training and comms & engagement plan by end Aug ◑
  - Action: Program underway with Ops Transformation consultant
- KR: Recognize, reward, excite and retain our top talent – zero loss in Platinum talent over the half ◑

Stepping back out of the details:

> **A DELIBERATE MOS GIVES YOU A PROACTIVE WAY TO MANAGE INFORMATION, COLLABORATION, AND ACTIONS TO MOVE YOUR KEY RESULTS FORWARD. THIS ALSO HELPS YOU ELIMINATE "MEETINGS FOR THE SAKE OF MEETINGS."**

I like to revise my MOS every six months, as a proactive hygiene check-in. We all have meetings that are painful and ineffective but have been around forever and become part of the company culture, so everyone is scared to question why you're having them. Vaporizing your MOS every six months means there are no sacred cows, and that you give the team equal right to question every meeting and interaction for its effectiveness.

I set up recurring meetings for twelve- or twenty-six-week cycles. When these end, it's time to look at whether the meeting was effective before setting up another series.

RUNNING EFFECTIVE MEETINGS

Being able to run effective and engaging meetings (and workshops, for that matter)—to rally a group around a problem—is critical to effective strategy execution. For every meeting in your MOS, it's worth defining the "Q and 5Ps" (**question, purpose, payoffs, participants, preparation**, and **process**) so everyone stays aligned on what the meeting is for. As you roll out your MOS, you can include the Q&5Ps in meeting invites and flash them up on the screen at the start of each meeting while people find their feet. Here are some thoughts and reflections across the Q&5Ps of meeting and workshop planning:

Question

Having a few (one to three) guiding questions for your meeting is incredibly useful. Ask yourselves:

WHAT QUESTION(S) ARE WE HERE TO ANSWER?

If you don't need to answer anything, then you aren't there to make decisions. If you aren't there to make decisions, then the meeting should have been an email/dashboard/text message!

Purpose

Now, I appreciate that this links directly to the "questions" prompt above. However, it is still worth phrasing "purpose" (and the other Ps) in response to a few key questions:

Why are you having the meeting? What is the situation and complication underpinning the meeting? The meeting might be a:

- Monthly performance review to capture learnings and ensure you are on track for the next cycle, or a

- Project meeting to review progress and ensure the critical path is clear of obstacles.

Payoffs

What do *you* want to get out of the meeting? What do you want others to get out of it?

Here, think hearts, minds, and actions. What information do you need to share and grapple with to put people's minds at ease? How do you want people to feel leaving the meeting? What actions do you want to drive as next steps?

Be sure to have a good balcony view on the above. Is the meeting to review performance and pull out blockers and learnings? To celebrate success and recognize good performance? Is it a forward-looking planning meeting? To inspire change and motivate? Are you here to give the group a reality check, leaving them feeling stressed but hopeful? Are you here to celebrate and innovate? Solve a problem, come up with a plan, and inspire joint hard work?

Each of these would inform a different tone, process, and toolset for your meeting.

Participants

Informed by the above, who should you have in the meeting? Who can contribute? Who needs to make decisions? Who should be part of the process to buy into the outcomes and next steps? Who can add gravitas and authority? Do you need that? Who can add specialist perspectives or knowledge?

Crafting the group is important.

Preparation

I don't need to tell you that preparation is key. In the context of meetings, here are some questions to consider:

- How do you want people to prepare offline, before the meeting? What information can they absorb to better prepare for discussions and problem solving in the meeting?

- Are there any other meetings or one-on-ones that are best had before the meeting in question, to ensure participants have the necessary information for the discussion?

- Do you even want people to be prepared for a particular meeting?

An important component of preparation and process is to be clear on what you need to discuss and problem solve in the room. Information sharing and updates can happen via email and dashboards. Pre-reads are gold (if they're succinct).

ENSURING YOUR PREPARATION AND PROCESS ARE MARRIED TO THE QUESTIONS YOU ARE GATHERED TO ANSWER IS THE KEY TO RUNNING AN EFFECTIVE MOS.

Process

This is a massively neglected part of the puzzle. You do everything else, then get in a room and start talking.

Who should chair the meeting? Should it be facilitated? Who is best positioned to keep everyone on track, but not "take over" the meeting?

Start with brief context setting. Even if everyone knows why they're there, it helps them slip into the right mental gear. Give a succinct and powerful, top-down "why we're here" introduction. Cover purpose and payoff for sure. This creates common ground and subconsciously rallies the room around a shared goal.

Decide what framework you want to use to center the meeting on. This is "the page" or question or problem-solving tool that you are getting everyone around. Some tips:

- **Progress review**: use an appropriate dashboard of metrics and a template to drive synthesis of qualitative inputs.

- **Planning**: use a Gantt chart.

- **Prioritization**: use a prioritization matrix.

- **Problem solving a complex strategic question**: use a problem statement and an issue tree.

Now, no matter how well you design and set up your meeting, *if the levels of discussions are shit, your MOS is shit*. Which brings me to my next point:

SYNTHESIS AND TOP-DOWN COMMUNICATION

To get the most out of your MOS, individual meetings, and any other engagement, people need to communicate effectively. A vast portion of my interventions involve clarifying and synthesizing what people are trying to say. Without you around to "cut through the crap," it's invaluable to drive structured communication in the management team.

GREAT COMMUNICATION DOESN'T MAGICALLY HAPPEN. IT'S GREAT BECAUSE IT'S DELIBERATE.

Synthesis versus summary

Nothing drives more management inefficiency than an inability to synthesize information. If you want effective focus, an effective MOS, and effective problem solving, train and coach your team to synthesize! Note that a synthesis is not the same thing as a summary:

Summary—An abridged version of the original. The same information but in shorter form.

Synthesis—Insight. What is the information telling me? What is the "so-what?"

Example:

Summary: *The initial discovery and design activities took a week longer than we had anticipated. This seems to have been incorrectly scoped in the initial sales process. We are working on increasing capacity in the project team—specifically the engineers—to speed up the implementation phase.*

Synthesis: *Shit happens, but we will still deliver the project on time. The surprises couldn't have been seen by the sales team.*

If someone gives you a summary, *you* must do the work to synthesize it. And with incomplete information, you may draw the wrong conclusions or insights.

SYNTHESIS ADDS VALUE. SYNTHESIS IS THE EXECUTIVE ANSWER TO "SO WHAT?" AND "WHAT'S NEXT?" EMPLOYEES ARE PAID FOR SUMMARIES. MANAGERS ARE PAID FOR SYNTHESIS.

Be a synthesizer, not a summarizer.

The elevator pitch

You may have heard of this idea, but few people appreciate the second-order insights. First, the premise behind the concept is:

> *You arrive at work. You get into the elevator. Just as the doors are about to close, the CEO walks in and says, "How is it going with X?" You now have twenty-two floors or thirty seconds to give the CEO your synthesis.*

The idea is to force top-down insight delivery. What does the CEO care about? What is the headline? What will have impact? Time is money, so get to the point.

Where I see people get second-order insight wrong is that they *try to summarize*, and get caught up in trying to communicate all the relevant information in as few words as possible. When someone gives me a good elevator pitch, it's because *they know what the key insight is*. If you are crystal clear in your mind on what the key insight is, you can give an elevator pitch in your sleep.

> *"The project has had its speed bumps but will be delivered on time. There is nothing we need to systemically fix from the learnings."*

AN ELEVATOR PITCH IS A PROBLEM-SOLVING TOOL. IT'S A LIFESTYLE. IT'S BEING ON TOP OF WHAT THE HELL IS GOING ON IN YOUR SPHERE OF THE BUSINESS AND WHY THAT MATTERS—THE "SO-WHATS."

If your managers always have a good elevator pitch in their minds, it means they know what the key insights are! It means they are on the problem-solving balcony. Stepping back and coming up for air daily, weekly, and monthly—to distill the elevator pitches of what's going on in their spheres of the business—is key to being in control, and key to driving the right "what's next."

Senior managers maintaining their balcony views is what drives rapid progress and growth. Synthesis puts a MOS on steroids.

STRATEGIC PROBLEM SOLVING

Poor problem solving is probably the most systemic challenge I see in every type of business, big and small. This includes:

· Knowing what to do but not how to do it.

· Not identifying root cause blockers effectively.

· Not communicating effectively during problem solving.

· Not solving the right problem.

It's incredible how much rapid progress you can make if you problem solve effectively. Here is a classic example of how strategic problem solving goes wrong:

I was a strategic advisor for an executive team. As in a lot of my consulting work, I was very hands-on to make sure I knew what was really happening at different levels in the org and could give better, more impactful strategic input. I was invited to an executive meeting, and was sent an agenda. The third point on the agenda read: "Sales Strategy Presentation." I knew immediately it was going to be a nightmare.

Max was the sales manager. He was an intermediate manager, and had a lot to learn. I knew how this was going to play out. Max was a "sales guy." He would have put a ton of work into this sales strategy presentation, wanting to impress the executives and shine.

From the first slide, it was clear that:

· *Max had put a lot of time into this.*

· *Max was missing some seriously important aspects of a sales strategy, and hadn't included some important considerations of the business strategy.*

· *Max had worked on this alone.*

Now, this was a real clusterfuck, for three associated reasons:

- *Max had not only wasted a lot of time, but was also now extremely emotionally attached to this presentation. It was a "presentation" and not a draft. This was not a working session. It was now in a position where he wanted appreciation and recognition—a "good job."*

- *Lack of a structured process meant that Max hadn't uncovered obvious blind spots in thinking. Had he followed a structured, strategic problem-solving process, he could have uncovered them himself. Had he even Googled "sales strategy" and looked at a couple of contents pages, he would have had a better executive view.*

- *Lack of collaboration, especially with more strategic thinkers, meant that Max's answer was shit and his time and effort poorly spent, and he couldn't use any of the team as co-sponsors and proponents of his strategy.*

Overall, this put everyone else in a very difficult position. *Do we accept a crap strategy, so that we don't hurt Max's feelings? How do we give feedback while tiptoeing around his pride? Where am I going to find time to deal with this unnecessary emotional fallout due to a poor problem-solving strategy?*

When this kind of behavior compounds on a project, you stand to lose months and months of progress.

> USE THE RIGHT PROBLEM-SOLVING APPROACH TO KEEP MINDS AND EFFORTS FOCUSED, TO LEARN THE RIGHT LESSONS QUICKLY, AND TO GET TO THE CRUX OF ISSUES FAST. THIS WILL SIGNIFICANTLY ACCELERATE YOUR FOUNDER-FREEING PROJECTS AND BUSINESS GROWTH.

Diverge, then converge

A good overall philosophy to problem solving is to not fixate on finding a solution at the outset. It sounds crazy, but this is the foundation of efficient strategic problem solving. Strategic problems are big, hairy, and multifaceted. Jumping in with assumptions or blinkered solutions, only to find out later that a huge part of the thinking was absent, is such a waste of time.

Problems are complicated. Strategic problems have contexts and perspectives and angles to them. Scenarios. Forces. You need to take the time to adequately diverge, explore, and learn. It can take days, maybe weeks. It's a mindset, not a time frame. Good diverging can happen in one well-run project kickoff session.

Then, you need to converge and narrow down to find some solutions. Having a common strategic problem-solving framework—along with its language, process, and tools—will ensure the team maintains discipline, collaborates effectively, and doesn't fall into old habits.

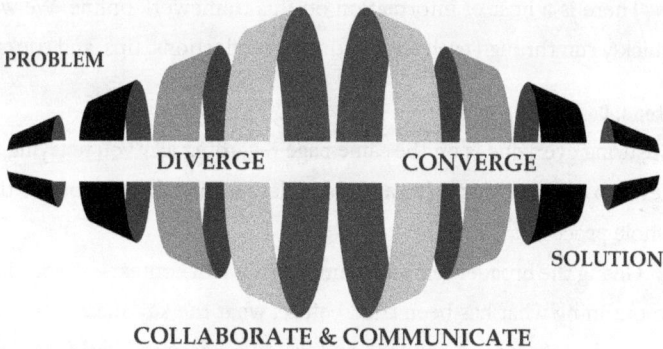

PROBLEM

DIVERGE   CONVERGE

SOLUTION

COLLABORATE & COMMUNICATE

A seven-step problem-solving process[9]

McKinsey's tried and tested seven-step system is a great structured process for tackling even the most complex strategic problems. Key principles from each of the discrete steps, applied to your Top 3 | 10 Hitlist, will drive rapid progress.

Here are the steps:

· Define the problem

· Structure the problem

· Prioritize the focus areas

· Work plan

9   https://www.mckinsey.com/capabilities/strategy-and-corporate-finance/our-insights/how-to-master-the-seven-step-problem-solving-process

- Analyze
- Synthesize
- Develop recommendations and actions

Inherent to McKinsey's seven steps is the concept of "diverge and then converge," which we just touched on. You spend significant time defining and structuring the problem, exploring the different aspects of the problem, and seeing how others have approached and tackled the problem. Then, you apply your mind and prioritize where you believe the greatest value lies. And then, you go solve stuff and take action!

There is a host of information on this framework online. We will quickly run through each step, with short reflections, tips, and tricks.

Step 1: Define the problem

Ensuring everyone is on the same page regarding *why* you're trying to develop a strategy or solve a problem lays a solid foundation for the whole process.

Giving the broader team a common ground of context—in addition to outlining what has been tried before, what the key success factors are, and what success will look and feel like—accelerates the process and yields great results.

I'm sure, as a Founder, that you've been caught off-guard by how blinkered some people's views of the business and its moving parts are. As Founder, you're often expected to keep a lot of balls in the air—balls from across the business, as well as the connections between them. In contrast, most managers only see one or two balls.

GETTING THE KEY PEOPLE INVOLVED IN A PROBLEM OR STRATEGY INTO A ROOM, AND GETTING ALL THE BALLS ON THE TABLE, GIVES EVERYONE THE "FOUNDER'S VIEW" FROM THE START!

A good kickoff would include rich discussions around strategic context, scope, criteria for success, key stakeholders and processes, barriers to impact, and so on. You would then capture all of this into a guiding problem statement to keep everyone aligned (a SMART one).

As you can tell from many of these aspects, there is a lot you won't know upfront. But getting a collective download of what you do know, getting on the same page, and putting explicit pins in the important things you need to learn ASAP gives the team an aligned, running start.

Step 2: Structure the problem

As we saw with Max, if you head out of the starting blocks and only cover one element of the problem, remaining oblivious to the other (possibly more valuable or complex) parts of the problem, you will come unstuck.

Real innovation, real gear shifts, happen when you approach a problem with the broadest lens possible, and with a rigorous, structured approach. *Structuring a problem is probably the hardest and most valuable step in the process.* This is your chance to look for really distinctive solutions and opportunities.

Issue trees are "structured mind maps"—they structure thinking into buckets and branches that strive to cover as much of the problem as possible. Below is an actual issue tree I used for a go-to-market strategy for a new product. While there are some overlaps and missing elements in this example, I want you to take note of one important thing:

ISSUE TREES ALLOW YOU TO READ MY MIND! THEY GIVE COMPLETE CLARITY—WITHIN TWO MINUTES—OF HOW I AM THINKING ABOUT THE PROBLEM. THEY LET YOU SEE THE BIG BUCKETS OF THINKING, AND IMMEDIATELY PICK UP ON IF I HAVE MISSED SOMETHING.

Can you appreciate how this both improves the rigor of problem solving *and* drastically improves and accelerates collaboration?

Note: the issue tree is not a planning tool—it isn't focusing on asking, "What do we have to do?" The issue tree is a structured mapping of your response to the question, "What are the different things we should think about and how do they relate?" *In doing so, you are diverging and covering the whole problem.*

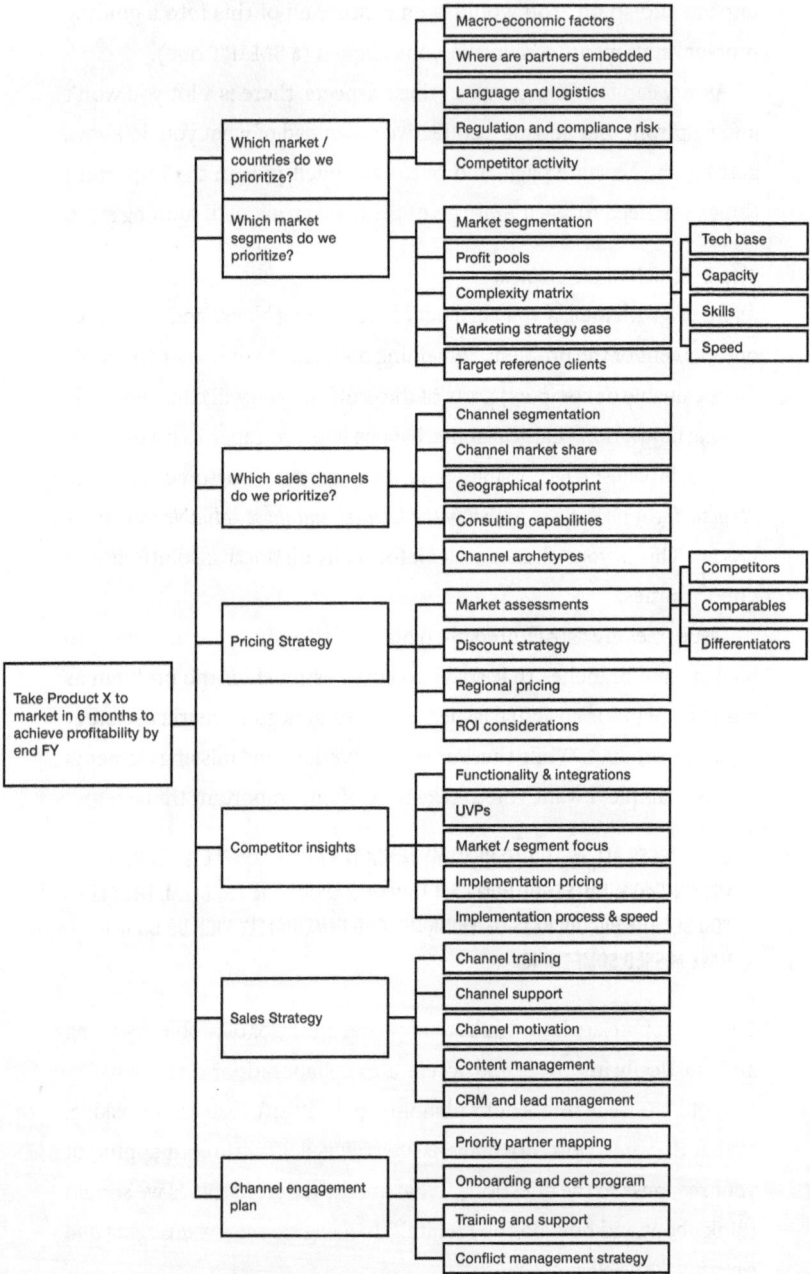

```
Take Product X to market in 6 months to achieve profitability by end FY
│
├── Which market / countries do we prioritize?
│     ├── Macro-economic factors
│     ├── Where are partners embedded
│     ├── Language and logistics
│     ├── Regulation and compliance risk
│     └── Competitor activity
│
├── Which market segments do we prioritize?
│     ├── Market segmentation
│     ├── Profit pools
│     ├── Complexity matrix ──── Tech base
│     │                          Capacity
│     │                          Skills
│     │                          Speed
│     ├── Marketing strategy ease
│     └── Target reference clients
│
├── Which sales channels do we prioritize?
│     ├── Channel segmentation
│     ├── Channel market share
│     ├── Geographical footprint
│     ├── Consulting capabilities
│     └── Channel archetypes
│
├── Pricing Strategy
│     ├── Market assessments ──── Competitors
│     │                           Comparables
│     │                           Differentiators
│     ├── Discount strategy
│     ├── Regional pricing
│     └── ROI considerations
│
├── Competitor insights
│     ├── Functionality & integrations
│     ├── UVPs
│     ├── Market / segment focus
│     ├── Implementation pricing
│     └── Implementation process & speed
│
├── Sales Strategy
│     ├── Channel training
│     ├── Channel support
│     ├── Channel motivation
│     ├── Content management
│     └── CRM and lead management
│
└── Channel engagement plan
      ├── Priority partner mapping
      ├── Onboarding and cert program
      ├── Training and support
      └── Conflict management strategy
```

Step 3: Prioritize the focus areas

Once the team have their heads around the problem and have really diverged, it's time to prune the tree and decide what to take forward to be analyzed. Here, you generally use a classic two-by-two matrix:

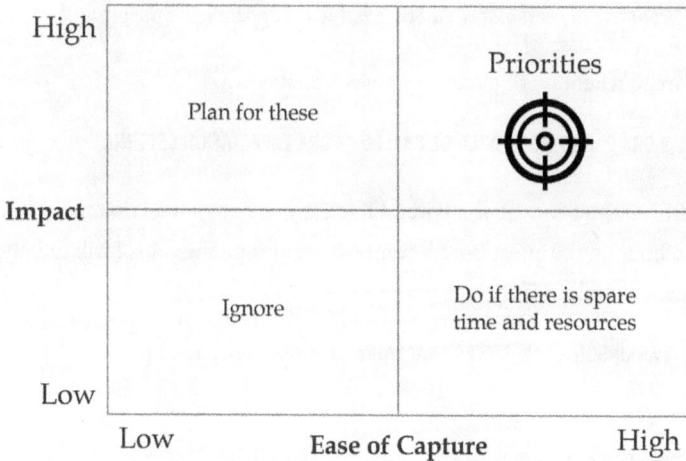

Don't work out the impact to the nth degree here—quick-and-dirty, back-of-the-envelope calculations will help you get a good initial view of your matrix. Use the team, preferably in an engaging way, to seek your most directionally accurate view.

Step 4: Work plan

This is by far the most neglected step in management and problem solving. Let me give you an example of why this is a problem:

> *In a meeting, an executive says to the business development manager, "I heard that MDX is aggressively targeting Canada. Will you please look into that for our next session?"*

> *Four weeks pass, and the team enters their next business development review session.*

First on the agenda is "Review of Canada as a Strategic Target." The slide count at the bottom of the screen says "1 of 82" slides. It becomes clear that the BDM and their team have spent the better part of two weeks deeply interrogating Canada as a business development target.

All the executive expected was a couple of phone calls to their Canadian contacts to get a quick read on what was happening on the ground.

This is where work planning comes into its own.

WORK PLANNING SHOULD BE CALLED "WORK EXPECTATION SETTING."

If I want the two-hour answer, I'll tell my team to spend no more than an hour on the question. If I want a few quick phone calls, I will tell my team to make a few quick phone calls.

PARKINSON'S LAW STATES THAT WORK EXPANDS TO FILL THE TIME ALLOCATED TO IT.

Yes, a work plan may be out of date in a couple of days as things change and learnings are incorporated. But proactively managing the team's expectations on how they spend their precious time and attention is fundamental to productivity.

Step 5: Analyze
You're no doubt familiar with Step 5: do the research, have the interviews, build the model, run a focus group. Whatever it is, here you are doing a deep dive into the priority elements of the problem in line with how you have agreed to plan your work.

Step 6: Synthesize
As you complete your analyses, you ask, "So what?"

What do you do with these results? What insights are they giving you? What actions could you take? How do they relate to other insights you have gained to build a strategic picture?

Step 7: Develop recommendations and action plans

Lastly, you structure all your insights into a holistic strategy, concrete actions plans, and compelling communications to move everyone in the desired direction.

> HAVING AN EXPLICIT PROBLEM-SOLVING APPROACH, KNOWING WHERE THE TEAM IS IN THE PROCESS, AND ENSURING EACH STEP IS GIVEN ITS DUE CARE AND DILIGENCE WILL GIVE YOU PEACE OF MIND THAT THE BEST SOLUTIONS ARE FOUND AND THE RICHEST PROPOSAL FORMULATED.

Applying a rigorous project and problem-solving approach to your Top 3 | 10 Hitlist will save you months and unlock significantly more value than a non-deliberate approach.

Coach, coach, coach

Leadership styles and communication styles are intricately linked. However, *synthesis, top-down communication, and problem solving can be trained and coached.* Instilling a coaching and feedback culture around these key elements, as part of the SHIFT™ program, is a golden opportunity. Observe yourself and your team members! Record meetings, presentations, and town hall speeches for your team and company. Watch them together to give contextual feedback and look for opportunities. It sounds scary, but it's actually incredibly fun and effective.

> MOST OF ALL, IF SOMEONE ISN'T SYNTHESIZING, ASK THEM TO! THIS IS AS SIMPLE AS ASKING, "CAN YOU PLEASE GIVE US THE SO-WHAT?"

Think of the hours your business will save across all meetings over a year if people knew their point and got to it sooner. **Encouraging people and holding them accountable to *focus* on the "so-what" will accelerate everything!**

If someone is presenting solutions without a "Project Kickoff to Define the Problem," tell them to schedule one!

Pulling together "Strategy," "Harmony," and "Improve" into a "Focused" management operating system—with top-notch communicators focusing on strategic insights—unlocks significant opportunities for growth and hassle-free business management. Now, it's time for the final step in the SHIFT™ Business Operating System: let's make sure everyone stays on **TARGET**.

FOCUS TO-DO LIST

☐ Best-practice management systems and structures, including a business performance dashboard, are in place for the management team to keep their eyes on their OKRs and Top 3 | 10 Hitlist. They don't get lost in the weeds, and they don't need herding and redirection from you, the Founder.

☐ A cohesive and granular management operating system has been implemented to ensure the right information is shared, to make the right decisions and trigger the right strategic problem solving, efficiently and effectively.

☐ The management team has a deliberate monthly beat to ensure information cascades, conversations are optimized, and engagements are well-orchestrated.

☐ Each meeting or engagement has a well-thought-through set of 5Ps to make sure the management team spends time wisely, and focuses on the right questions, topics, and actions.

☐ The team has been trained and coached to communicate effectively, to draw out insights, and to efficiently engage in a top-down manner. This keeps everyone's heads above water and gets them to the point sooner.

☐ The team collaborates using a joint strategic problem-solving framework. They follow the process and use the tools diligently to quickly come up with effective and innovative solutions to strategic problems.

CHAPTER 7
TARGET

*"The best way to predict the future is
to create it. A strong performance culture
empowers individuals to do just that."*

– PETER DRUCKER

A strong performance culture unites people around a cause, and their individual contributions to that cause. You now have your cause ("Strategy") and your OKRs ("Harmony"). You have given your team the best ways to work ("Improve") and the management systems to maintain your efforts on what matters ("Focus").

You now need to get the most out of this system (delivery, feedback, and opportunities) by driving a performance culture.

Specifically, a performance culture that isn't built on you, the Founder, running around herding the team.

A strong day-to-day performance culture is driven through targets. Targets are the final link in the chain, and, often, the last mile of delivery that I find missing in businesses.

Each individual in the broader team must know what they need to deliver in order to support and drive the OKRs (and, hence, strategy) of the business, and *want* to deliver it. From the moment a team member enters the office, that is what they should be thinking about:

"How do I deliver X today so that I can deliver Y this week?"

"What can we do to make delivering X easier?"

"I know if I deliver X plus 10%, I will be rewarded."

There are three key facets to a performance culture that you need to implement so that the team becomes self-driven and self-motivating, moving in the right direction without their trusty old cheerleader (you). They are:

- Purpose and targets
- Compensation and incentives
- Performance management

PURPOSE AND TARGETS

In the medium to long term, you have business purpose and you have individual purpose.

I have yet to meet a Founder who doesn't care about their team. The problem is that this care can take the form of personal connection and close working relationships over more structural ways of linking business and personal purpose.

In reality, you seldom want your employees with the business for longer than, say, eight years. You need fresh energy and profiles, and your staff need fresh energy and challenges. So, "undying commitment to the Founder" is *not* a good purpose. Each person has aspirations, needs, and dreams, and their time with the business is just a chapter in their book. Your job, your opportunity, is to make that chapter meaningful for both the individual and the business.

The business has its own aspirations, needs, and dreams (or vision). We have distilled these into OKRs for each area of the business.

THE MORE YOU CAN CONNECT THE ASPIRATIONS, NEEDS, AND DREAMS OF THE BUSINESS WITH THOSE OF THE INDIVIDUAL EMPLOYEE, THE MORE YOU WILL GET EVERYONE FOCUSED AND COMMITTED TO THEIR HIGHEST CONTRIBUTION. YOU DO THIS THROUGH PURPOSE, TARGETS, AND CULTURE.

Targets

From your value drivers and "Improve" process mapping, you have identified the important outcomes and metrics for your core processes. Now, by considering the individual roles in the organization, you need to determine the KPIs that drive individuals to contribute to your OKRs.

Often there is more than one. As you will see in the next section, good KPIs encompass outputs, efficiency, effectiveness, values, and so on. There is seldom one KPI to rule them all.

But you want people to focus.

So, using your objectives and the key results for this quarter, you will need to focus on particular KPIs and what you want to move and improve. You then need to make these KPIs meaningful. You need to structurally link personal performance, personal development and purpose, and business performance to make everyone a "business owner."

PAY FAIRLY. PAY BONUSES. AND HELP PEOPLE ACHIEVE THEIR PERSONAL DREAMS.

Performance culture

This isn't a long section, because implementing SHIFT™ drives the core elements of culture in itself. However, your OKRs, MOS, targets, and personal purpose all dovetail into a performance culture.

The management team drives focus, energy, and hype, all structured around their OKRs. You motivate teams and individual staff, every week, to show up and drive performance for themselves, their teams, and the business. Your "Improve" efforts clear the way and empower your teams to deliver effectively.

Over and above this, *visible leadership and role modeling* is critical. Management needs to be singing from the same hymn sheet. The team needs to be recognizing and rewarding the right outcomes, as well as the enabling values and behaviors that drive those outcomes.

The team also needs to be role modeling and coaching the right values and behaviors that underpin good performance. For the common good, collaborative problem solving around poor performance is as critical as managing stress and resilience.

To achieve this, you need to proactively build management performance culture check-ins, working sessions, and problem-solving sessions into your MOS. OKR reviews, target setting, taglines, reward and recognition, and performance management—these are all clear agenda items in your monthly, quarterly, and annual beats, respectively.

Linked to this is fair compensation and incentives.

COMPENSATION AND INCENTIVES

Ah, the dark art of compensation.

You can find a million and one opinions online about compensation theories (mostly from human resources practitioners who don't manage ops people). Allow me to share my practical learnings and approach.

Every industry and business is different. The culture you're driving—the impact, contributions, layers, quality of managers, management styles, company culture, performance culture, and so on—has a significant bearing on your compensation philosophy. Non-corporate, Founder-led businesses often have the unique advantage of being able to provide an environment where people have more input, impact, and exposure. These are seldom captured and advertised.

Deliberately thinking through your business's employee value proposition (EVP)—and management value proposition (MVP), for that matter—is the foundation of any compensation framework.

WHAT PROFILES ARE YOU HIRING, INTO WHAT EMPLOYEE VALUE PROPOSITION, AGAINST WHICH TALENT COMPETITORS?

If you aren't competing with banks (and you shouldn't be), then you don't need to pay banking salaries. Understand this, codify this, and then quantify this.

What is your EVP? What are the direct- and indirect-benefit trade-offs? Where on the compensation benchmark spectrum should you be playing? Considering the solid citizens already in the business (who haven't left to go earn a banking salary), ask yourself, what's keeping them around? How well do you understand that?

All of this contributes to a fuzzy but deliberate picture that informs your compensation decisions. My advice, through all of this, is to be deliberate, fair, and transparent about the overall philosophy. Then, in application, you adjust for role criticality, performance, contributions to energy and culture, risk, role redundancy, and so on.

All of this is objectively codified into a compensation framework that the management team can drive forward—with guidance, but without you as the Founder calling all the shots. (And without any danger of Founder favoritism.)

Added on to base compensation are *traditional incentives*, like the performance bonus. In the next section, on performance management, we will talk about frontline operational incentives. Here, I am really talking about company-wide performance bonus philosophies. A couple of thoughts:

- I don't believe annual or semi-annual performance bonuses change Tom's get-up-and-go on a Monday morning. Similar to quitting smoking, those benefits are so far into the future that they aren't effective in changing short-term behavior by themselves.

- The benefits of performance bonuses are short-lived—psychologists have proved this.

- Performance bonuses are a ticket to play. Most companies offer them. If you don't, it will look weird.

- Performance bonuses are *rewards* and not incentives. They should be treated accordingly.

So, my suggestion is: don't get hung up on individual performance bonus philosophy. Have one. Keep it simple. In the context of "Freeing the Founder"—and the hype around unleashing business growth while freeing the Founder—a business performance–linked bonus pool is often a good idea.

Linked to your mission and goals, you would have budgeted some scenarios around performance and profits. One of the incredibly effective levers to drive a performance culture, teamwork, and a sense of belonging is to carve out a "bonus pool" from retained profits.

You can be quite deliberate about this, as highlighted in this example:

In one of the businesses I worked with, we built our one-pager business model and set some "benchmarks." If the business grew and achieved over $5 million in profits, the Founder was prepared to carve out one-third of the profits above $5 million to distribute to the staff (in proportion to their salary, to avoid complexity).

Ten percent growth would mean an extra $500,000 in profits. So, that would mean $160,000 extra that could be distributed to the staff for that year, over and above their standard comp and performance bonuses.

No promises we may not be able to keep. No growth, no cost. And everyone was in it together. Pretty elegant, and generous.

Over and above this: save your energy for purpose, targets, and performance management. After all, you want to be paying, rewarding, and embracing solid citizens. Poor performers should find more appropriate careers elsewhere.

PERFORMANCE MANAGEMENT

There are always a hundred excuses why managers don't manage performance. Ninety-nine of these hinge on fear of conflict and tough conversations. (Or Founders being too soft on their favorites.)

Regardless, performance management is so much more than dealing with "the bottom 10%." Performance management is also about purpose.

> A PERFORMANCE CULTURE IS ABOUT STAFF KNOWING THAT YOU CARE ABOUT HOW MUCH WORK THEY DO, BECAUSE THEIR WORK MATTERS.

Performance management is about *managing* performance. First, having a handle on what "good" looks like and how to get there; then, aligning the teams around targets and processes to be good, and to get better.

> PERFORMANCE MANAGEMENT IS NOT JUST "DEALING WITH THE BOTTOM 10%"–THAT IS LITERALLY 10% OF YOUR MANAGERS' JOBS. PERFORMANCE MANAGEMENT IS ABOUT DRIVING AND IMPROVING THE PERFORMANCE OF THE OTHER 90% THAT ARE ACTUALLY CONTRIBUTING!

By definition, firing the bottom 10% will make no difference to your business's performance and KPIs. Yes, it makes room for potential better performers, and, yes, it is your managers' jobs to relocate staff who are not upholding their side of the employment bargain. But if 90% of your focus is on the bottom 10%, then you aren't doing your jobs as leaders and managers.

The employee bell curve

Let's have a look at the bell curve:

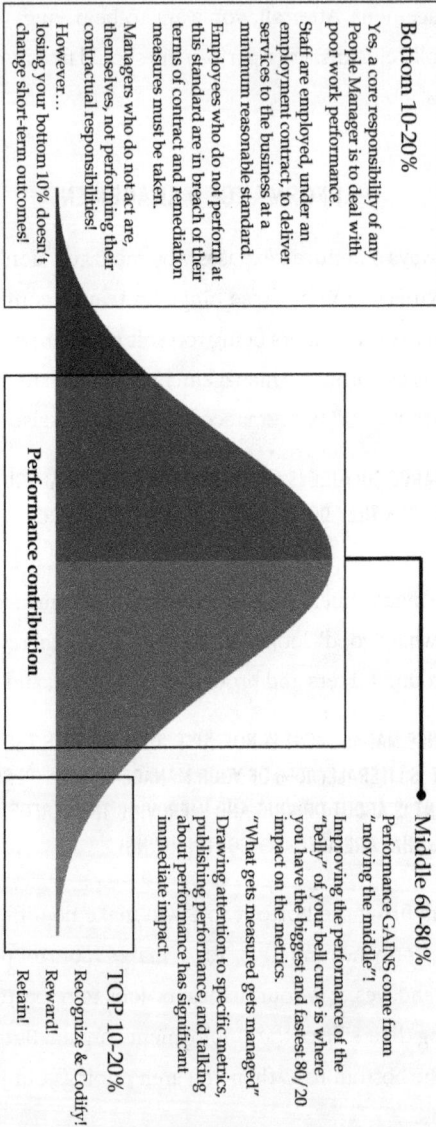

Bottom 10-20%

Yes, a core responsibility of any People Manager is to deal with poor work performance.

Staff are employed, under an employment contract, to deliver services to the business at a minimum reasonable standard.

Employees who do not perform at this standard are in breach of their terms of contract and remediation measures must be taken.

Managers who do not act are, themselves, not performing their contractual responsibilities!

However... losing your bottom 10% doesn't change short-term outcomes!

Performance contribution

Middle 60-80%

Performance GAINS come from "moving the middle"!

Improving the performance of the "belly" of your bell curve is where you have the biggest and fastest 80/20 impact on the metrics.

"What gets measured gets managed"

Drawing attention to specific metrics, publishing performance, and talking about performance has significant immediate impact.

TOP 10-20%

Recognize & Codify!
Reward!
Retain!

The bottom 20%

Either they are missing something, or they are in the wrong line of work. With the right performance management framework, you should figure that out with minimal effort.

Now, I'm not saying you should give up on your bottom 20%. Sometimes they need training, coaching, or support. Sometimes they just need some tough love and a kick in the pants to get moving. Here's an example:

I managed a bunch of call center operations at one point. Thillon was a salesperson and always an average to low performer. He kept to himself, and wasn't disruptive. He was quite introverted. He was contributing, but not shooting the lights out.

Then, randomly, his performance dropped below my performance management threshold. That meant that Thillon got to "have lunch with me in the boardroom." I was annoyed. He had shown he could do the job—I had listened to his sales calls—and for some reason was now choosing not to. I reined myself in and gave him the benefit of the doubt. Maybe his dog had died. Divorce. Who knows? Let's find out.

He had no good answers. He was flat. He wasn't improving. He wasn't earning enough. He was as disappointed as I was.

So, I gave him a stern talking-to. He had potential, but he was looking for someone else to give him the energy. He wasn't contributing to team culture. He was Eeyore in the corner, and it was showing in his performance and coming through on his calls. He had the tools, the training, and the support. He just didn't have himself.

I told him that he had one month to sort himself out, or he was packing up his desk. Two years later, Thillon became one of my best-ever sales managers.

Some people need to be shown the door, and some need to be shown the skylight. Don't break your back or waste your time, but *spend* some time. You never know what Thillons you could find.

The top 20%

The worst thing you can do with your top performers is leave them alone. Yes, they need reward and recognition—but they also need purpose. If I hear "You're great" all day long, I will a) believe you, and b) start thinking about my next challenge.

Also, be very careful about rewarding them with a promotion! Take the time to really understand what makes them tick and what makes them good. Sometimes great individual contributors make the worst people leaders. That's a very serious and scalable failure, and impossible to undo through a demotion.

When it comes to the top 20% of performers, you need to:

- hang on to them for as long as possible and have them contributing to the bottom line, and

- figure out what they are doing so you can get the middle 60 to 80% doing the same thing!

Keep your top 20% motivated and working hard, but also consider taking a couple of hours out of their week to build and disseminate best practices. Who better to create training content, FAQs, and practical standard operating procedures than your top performers? Upskill them in giving training and coaching. In doing all of this, you're acknowledging their prowess. You're giving them social recognition. You're giving them a new challenge. And, you are building invaluable IP to move the middle!

The middle 60%

This is your performance lever. Move the middle and you will have the greatest impact on your KPIs and bottom line.

You need to consider both skill and will:

- How do I assess what skill (or skills) each individual is missing to make them a top performer? How do I best teach/coach that skill? Can I?

- What tasks and approaches can we systematize, either in a system (technology) or in a standard operating procedure?

- Do they need more reward and recognition? Do they just need more general happiness? Is there something holding them back/annoying them that I can remove?

- Do they need consequences/accountability/fear to motivate them?

- Do I need to make an example of a poor performer?

Improving the performance of those in the middle—the "belly" of your bell curve—is where you have the biggest and fastest 80/20 impact on the metrics of your business.

A performance management program

A comprehensive performance management framework is important in ensuring transparent, objective, and effective identification and correction of poor performance. Without a solid framework, poor performance goes unnoticed or is tolerated for far longer than necessary. Not only does this directly impact business performance and growth, but it also impacts culture. Nothing annoys good performers more than watching poor performers being tolerated and paid a salary.

There are five key layers to an effective performance management program:

1. There are standards (poor, average, great).

2. The standards are reasonable.

3. Your staff understand the standards.

4. Your staff have the training, tools, and support to perform to standard.

5. There are *rewards, recognition, and consequences* related to achieving or not achieving the standard(s).

Let's discuss each layer in more detail.

There are standards

You need a way to measure performance. In some operations, this is easy (like in the case of a sales call center). For some roles, like a communications officer, it's really difficult. But you need to have a transparent and assessable standard to measure performance.

Some managers use complicated weighted algorithms. My advice: keep it simple. If your staff don't understand it or believe in it, it won't have the desired motivating effect.

What if the role is really complicated and the work very variable? This seldom applies to a large team or group of people, so deal with those by applying your mind and getting creative.

If you find a largish team with this problem, that generally points to poor operating strategy, or managers trying to make people's lives more interesting at the expense of performance transparency. Delineating responsibilities to make them more concentrated and transparent is the go here. You don't need 100% uniformity.

> **BEING ABLE TO CONSISTENTLY PREDICT AND MEASURE 50 TO 80% OF AN INDIVIDUAL EMPLOYEE'S WORK IS KEY FOR PERFORMANCE MANAGEMENT.**

Also, be careful about mis-incentives, where focusing on one performance measure undermines another. Returning to the call center example, here's how that can play out:

I had a sales manager who started a big performance drive based off of call volumes. "You have to make sixty calls a day, or else."

The result? Some of the call center agents found numbers that went to voicemail. They could call and leave a nice, lengthy voicemail that looked like a legit call on the system.

Bad metric. Bad performance standard.

We will look at the concept of holistic KPIs in the next section.

The standard(s) are reasonable

What level of performance is just not good enough? What is great? Often, operations managers want to figure this out from the bottom up. "If I sit down for eight hours non-stop, I can fold 1,000 paper airplanes, so 1,000 should be our daily target." Theoretically, yes. But shit happens. Meetings happen. Chats happen (good for culture!). Why don't you sit down for eight hours a day, five days a week, for three months straight, and then tell me what your daily average is.

The best way to set targets is to statistically analyze historic performance and do a bit of "What do you need to believe?" analysis on the bottom end. If Tom only folds four paper airplanes, what the hell was he doing all day? Was he in a meeting for seven hours and forty-five minutes?

> TARGET SETTING, LIKE PRICING STRATEGY, IS AN ART.

But don't get it wrong! If your poor-performance threshold is too low, then you're accepting poor performance. If it's unreasonably high, you are asking for legal issues and a lot of admin. You need to decide on a *reasonable* performance standard, which may require some trial and error.

Your staff understand the standard(s)

This is a combination of internal communication (hype to get buy-in) and training. Again, if you are the only one who understands the standards/targets, you won't have any impact. The more your staff (and management) understand, buy in to, and link standards to purpose and strategy, the greater the impact of your performance management program.

From a legal perspective (where it matters), I would have training on the entire framework, the targets, the tools, the support, the consequences and processes, and so on, and have my staff sign an attendance register.

Your staff have the training, tools, and support to perform to standard

This is where the top 20% comes in. The intent of the entire program is to improve performance. Your managers aren't doing their job if they don't understand what good performance looks like, and what underpins good performance. Codifying that into training, standard operating procedures, FAQs, and providing individual coaching is a key job for your managers.

Again, keep records of coaching and training. Clearly communicate where staff can find resources like SOPs, handbooks, and so forth. Let them know who they can ask for help. Make this part of your induction and performance management training. Have refreshers. Again, have an attendance register.

There are rewards, recognition, and consequences related to achieving or not achieving the standard(s)

And, finally, you actually execute. You dovetail your performance management program into your MOS. You train your team leaders on how to have effective standups.

There are positive and negative consequences to performance. You hold your managers accountable, and monitor their performance, with regard to how they execute, run, and maintain the performance management program.

Holistic KPIs

Targets and KPIs are very powerful.

> "WHAT GETS MEASURED GETS MANAGED—EVEN WHEN IT'S POINTLESS TO MEASURE AND MANAGE IT, AND EVEN IF IT HARMS THE PURPOSE OF THE ORGANIZATION TO DO SO."—PETER DRUCKER

When setting targets and KPIs, I like to think about five elements of performance:

1. Are you working hard? What is your activity and your output?
2. Are you working smart? Are you efficiently using inputs and time?
3. Are you working accurately? Are your outputs up to standard?

4. Are you looking at ways to improve how you do things?

5. Are you fun to work with? (At the very least, don't be an asshole.)

Incentivizing volume of work at the expense of quality is a problem. Incentivizing quality at the expense of precious resources is also a problem. Consider this example:

> *Let's say you operate in a sales environment where you only focus on number of sales. Tom does 100 sales, and Cindy does 120 sales. Cindy is the star, right?*

> *Well, if Tom is given 500 leads to make his 100 sales, while Cindy went through 1,000 leads to get her 120 sales, who is the star now?*

For every role and situation, you need to assess what is important. Specifically, you need to pinpoint the performance dynamics and set targets accordingly.

Personal trainers

Once you have your performance management framework in place, it's your team leaders' time to shine. *Proactive performance management* is what drives performance. The best analogy I have come up with to explain this is personal training:

> *I see a personal trainer three times a week. My personal trainer understands my overall goal and sets daily targets for our workouts.*

> *Now, imagine this wild scenario:*

> *My personal trainer sets my targets and designs my workouts. She sends them to me on the first of the month.*

> *We then meet on the last day of the month, and we talk about the fifteen workouts I missed and the days I did two pushup sets instead of three. She*

*is angry and shits on me. I'm now fat AND disappointed in myself. But I
promise to try harder next month.*

Insane, right? That's not what my personal trainer is paid for.

*She is at every workout. She holds me accountable for showing up on time
and in the right gear. She makes sure I warm up and that I know how to
do pushups properly. She stands next to me during the workout and makes
sure I do three sets of twelve.*

*She sets realistic targets and makes sure I've done all my sets in the rea-
sonably allotted time.*

YOUR TEAM LEADERS OR FRONTLINE SUPERVISORS ARE PERSONAL TRAINERS.

They need to set Tom's target for the week. They need to know how
Tom is doing through the week. They need to intervene on Wednesday
if it looks like Tom isn't going to finish his last set of pushups by Friday.

Your team leaders need to be equipped with the data, communication
skills, and MOS to proactively drive performance.

Standups are your personal training sessions

The point of standups is to keep things on track. This is where you
check in on the number of pushups everyone has done and make sure
they are finishing their sets.

I've seen standups get prescriptive and negatively impact a performance culture.

On a complex, high-velocity production line, it may be necessary to
have standups multiple times a day. In most workplaces, however, two
to three times a week should be ample to drive strong weekly performance within the team. Here's an example of a weekly kickoff standup:

Purpose: *To set clear, understood, and reasonable team and individual
priorities for the week.*

Participants: *Team lead and team members.*

Prep: *Check weekly and daily performance for last week. Check any absentees, disruptions, or events for this week. Set week's targets and focus areas by team member, and perform any work allocation triage to assist with catchup where needed.*

Payoff: *Proactive target setting and performance prioritization. Team members are clear on expectations and can ask for support if needed.*

Process: *Fifteen minutes maximum.*

I like to work with my managers to develop clear, best-practice run sheets for standups so that we drive consistency. We use these to train our team leaders using role plays.

	Objective	Time	Talking points
Check ins	Check in on the team's "vibe". Note anyone needing an energy boost through the day (e.g., feeling tired and lagging targets)	2 min	"Good morning everyone and welcome to [DAY]. When I call your name, please share one word to describe how you are feeling today."
Synthesize last week's performance (Mon) **Synthesize yesterday's performance (Wed/Fri)**	Take note of how well the team is doing versus targets. How are we tracking for the month? Overall, are we looking good or do we need to pull together and push? Were there any disruptions to ops that we need to make up for?	3 – 5 min	"Overall the team did really well on XXX area of work. In terms of our monthly targets, we are tracking well on A and B. We need to catch up on C and D if we want to end in the green. Remember, [Tom] was sick on Thursday last week so we have some ground to make up. We are expecting a system disruption on Wednesday for 2 hours so we are adjusting our weekly targets to cater for that."
Overall priorities for the day	What area of work is the overall focus and what is the overall target. "We are in this together"	2 min	Highlight which area of work is the biggest focus for the whole team (where is the team target lagging for the week). Note any reallocations of work to help the team catch up ("Claire, you are in the green, can you help Tom with his XXX this morning to catch up.")
Individual priorities for the day	Touch base on each individual. Recognize good work. Highlight any catch-up areas for focus. Give a daily target if needed.	5 min	Go around the room with each team member. Recognize good performance for a day / week. Highlight any issues. Align on any help or support needed. Set a target for the morning / day for focused catch up.

Reactive performance management

Let's return to the personal trainer analogy for a moment. Let's say that when I get to the end of the month, even though my personal trainer has tried their best to keep me in the green, I just can't do the *reasonable* number of pushups required of me. As a result, it's time for the PT to find a new client.

Formalizing poor-performance interventions is critical. So often, I see team leaders taking an empathetic approach of "Ah, it's okay. Try again next month." This is a) too soft, and b) too informal.

> **STRING THREE "TRY AGAIN" MONTHS TOGETHER AND YOU HAVE ACCEPTABLE POOR PERFORMANCE.**

Then, when you try to act on it, you are effectively being unfair. Why was this performance level acceptable for three months and now "suddenly" you want to act on it and enforce consequences?

There *has* to be consistent and formalized escalation and interventions for poor performance in order for the process to work. These processes should always be well documented, by managers who are adequately trained, and supported by the relevant human resources or employee relations representative. Something like:

Step 1: Formal, documented coaching conversation with agreed, reasonable next steps and support.

Step 2: Support and performance documented. Formal, documented coaching with a warning.

Step 3: New career search.

Again, pull just one person into a Step 1 coaching session and often that is enough to get everyone on their toes. Some staff need a formal coaching session every three months to keep them on their toes. Whatever it takes, take staff that are in the "red" and either get them to green or let them go.

REWARD AND RECOGNITION

Compensation and incentives, as discussed earlier, are more long-term, structural mechanisms of "paying" staff for their work and contributions, and they apply to all staff. Reward and recognition are more discretionary, short-term mechanisms, applying to a small portion of the team who have shot the lights out.

The primary aim of a performance management framework is to drive and improve performance. Recognizing and rewarding good performance (and significant improvements in performance) is a core part of this framework, and reinforces a culture of employee value and appreciation.

YOU DO NOT INCENTIVIZE PEOPLE TO DO THEIR JOB.

One of the first things that managers ask for when you start talking about performance management is incentives. What I hear is something along the lines of:

Manager: "If we have a big enough carrot then I don't have to do my job as a manager. Everyone will be magically self-motivated."

Founder: "Great. How about I fire you and use your salary as a big fat carrot?"

As we discussed earlier, staff are paid their salaries (and benefits) in return for doing their job—that is, delivering in accordance with a reasonable standard. Significant contributions over and above that? Now, we can talk about rewards and recognition.

When you recognize, you recognize good performance. You recognize improvements in the middle. You recognize contributions to best practices and coaching.

As with everything in business, remember to get creative. (More on this in a moment.)

What to avoid: Tom is our star performer. Every month he gets first prize. There is no doubt that next time he will get first prize. Tom is happy. Everyone hates Tom.

Yes, Tom should be rewarded. Commission, bonuses, love and cuddles, whatever. But you also need rewards for "Most improved," or "Team player of the month," or "Best problem solver."

Where appropriate, a variable pay portion or commission is always useful to directly reward staff for improvements in performance. But remember, that also allows staff to choose their level of "happy average." Commission is not a self-fulfilling driving force. Managers still need to do their jobs. Targets still need to be set.

Over and above monetary rewards, there are prizes and the like. In my book *From Manager to Executive*,[10] I detailed what a staff dream program could look like. This is a great way to tap into the personal motivations of your team members and tailor your incentives and rewards to have maximum impact.

Here are some ideas:

We ran a performance push around springtime. My manager set up this whole "beach starter kit" with a beach cabana, deck chairs, beach blanket, towels, and an ice box with a six-pack of beers and a six-pack of Coke.

The most improved performer who "found new life" (spring theme) would win this.

It was awesome. It looked awesome. It made everyone think about the beach. It was front and center in the office, all day, every day, for a month.

---

[10] https://www.amazon.com/Manager-Executive-Take-Career-Level-ebook/dp/B0CW1N-1VWD

Then there was the "double-door fridge" incentive. My one manager assured me that staff went bananas for a double-door fridge, "even if they don't have space for it at home."

So, there we were—with a massive double-door fridge tied in a massive red bow. For a month.

The team broke records that month.

Get creative.

Individual versus team

On the question of individual incentives versus team incentives, I would say that it depends on the nature of the work, focus, and behavior you want to drive.

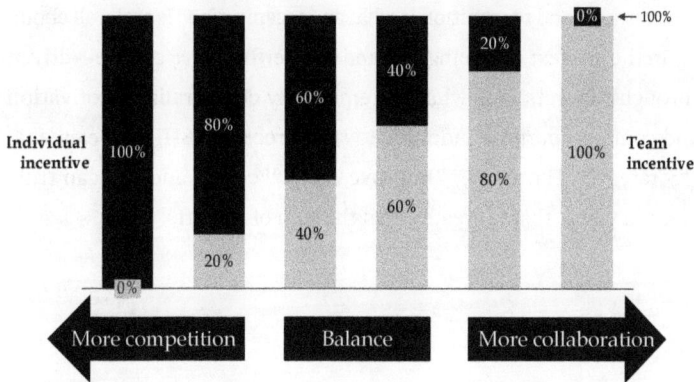

Individual targets combined with team targets and incentives is always a great middle ground. It drives individual accountability while leveraging the cover and support of the team to help upskill a challenged individual and make up for their low performance. Team leader boards, bragging rights, and monthly "lunch out" awards are a great dovetail into performance management programs.

One overarching rule about performance management and incentives is to shake them up often. Like business structures, a performance management framework can get boring. Consistently average performers can lose hope of ever improving on that particular KPI. Half yearly, if not quarterly, review the program and bring in some fresh thinking and approaches to drive excitement (and hope).

> **EVERYONE SEEKS PURPOSE. A PERFORMANCE CULTURE MEANS YOUR CONTRIBUTION MATTERS, AND YOU WILL BE RECOGNIZED AND REWARDED ACCORDINGLY.**

Aligning direction, structures, roles, objectives, improvements, and management focus means very little if the person on the frontline isn't doing the best they can, or is distracted. Giving your team members an individual purpose, giving them the tools and support they need to deliver your strategy and achieve your mission, and sharing in the business rewards and recognition is what an "organization" is really all about.

In the context of freeing a Founder, a performance culture—driven through "Targets"—is what systematically decentralizes motivation and common purpose. Add this to your preceding SHIFT™ elements ("Strategy," "Harmony," "Improve," and "Focus") and you can truly create a whole that is greater than the sum of its parts.

TARGET TO-DO LIST

- ☐ Staff are directed, incentivized, and rewarded to focus on the right things and do their best.

- ☐ The business has a formal compensation framework that accounts for the nature and size of the business, talent competition, and the employee value proposition of the company.

- ☐ As you change and evolve, you have an appropriate macro incentive or reward plan so your team shares in your big successes.

- ☐ Your team members are clear on their KPIs and their targets. They focus their attention and their efforts on these, and you have structure mechanisms to keep these top of mind.

- ☐ Your performance management framework and training empower your people leaders to recognize and reward top performers, codify best practices, and address poor performance in a constructive but effective way.

- ☐ You have a creative reward and recognition program that drives appropriate short-term excitement and energy to improve personal performance across both skill and will.

CONCLUSION:
LEADING THE SHIFT™

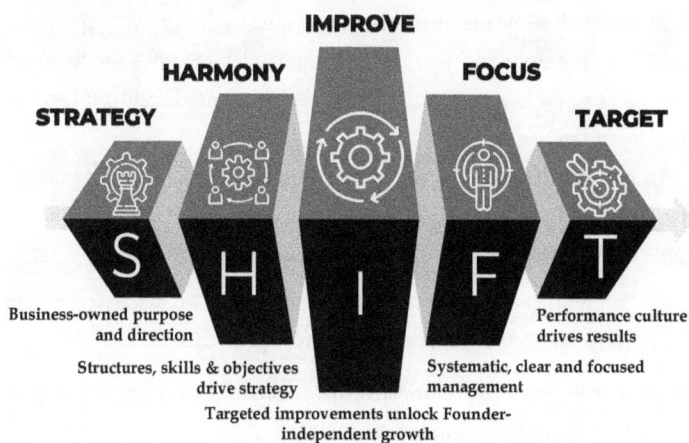

IMPROVE

HARMONY

STRATEGY

FOCUS

TARGET

S H I F T

Business-owned purpose
and direction

Performance culture
drives results

Structures, skills & objectives
drive strategy

Systematic, clear and focused
management

Targeted improvements unlock Founder-
independent growth

With SHIFT™, the whole becomes greater than the sum of the parts—making you, the Founder, a part of the story, not the star of the show.

Once you have driven the business through its first SHIFT™, from top to bottom, it becomes an ecosystem of facets that work in concert to refine and refocus performance at all levels. For example:

TARGET to **IMPROVE**—Operational performance management triggers ideas for improvements to structures, systems, processes, product, and so on. These feed into your strategic projects funnel for prioritization and resourcing.

FOCUS to **STRATEGIZE**—Learnings through your effective management operating system feed into your quarterly strategic reviews, and inform business and operations strategy iterations. You adjust key results and reallocate resources across functions (**HARMONIZE**).

Keep SHIFT™ explicitly in mind at the boardroom table to be sure you aren't forgetting about a key strategy execution lever and that the sections of your orchestra are coming in on time.

This operating model drives strong business structure across strategy, strategy execution, and strategic continuous improvement. This frees you, the Founder, from the business. Having strategic clarity and alignment will allow the business to continue to deliver with new leadership. As the Founder, you can choose to play an advisory or board role. Start a new business. Sail a yacht to the Canary Islands. Whatever your heart desires.

In my experience, success comes quickly. With renewed energy, structure, and focused action, quick wins deliver in months. Here are some of the wins I've helped businesses achieve:

- Remember the financial services business we discussed in the introduction? It experienced fivefold growth in six months.

- A fifty-person tech company experienced 25% year-on-year growth from year one of implementation.

- A process outsourcing client experienced a 14% increase in their key process line in four months.

- The first car dealership my automotive tech startup bought was number one in the country within three months.

Most importantly, these wins came at the same time as Founders were being freed and leadership structures were changing.

FINAL TIPS FOR REAL SUCCESS

As the Founder and current conductor of the orchestra, it is imperative that you are committed to the SHIFT™ and lead it wholeheartedly.

> ONE OF MY MANAGERS ALWAYS USED TO SAY, "A FISH ROTS FROM THE HEAD."

Here are some final considerations to drive success:

Get the whole SHIFT™ working

The five elements of the SHIFT™ Business Operating System are crucial to your successful "exit" from your business—so you *must* implement all five.

Having a great **STRATEGY** but no systematic way to execute it effectively (**HARMONY** and **IMPROVE**) leaves too much to you, the Founder, to coordinate. Having no systematic way to drive alignment and clarity in the management system (**FOCUS**) also leaves too much to you to coordinate. Having your **TARGET** frameworks and programs in place ensures the frontline is locked in and delivering without the need for you to conduct the orchestra.

The system works because it's a system. The faster you can get all of the elements spun up and working for you, the sooner the business (and you as the Founder) will reap the benefits of the system. Any gaps will put undue pressure on the other elements and start eroding the whole operating system.

To quote Voltaire, the perfect is the enemy of the good. Knowing what "good enough" looks like in the context of your unique business is the art. Enlisting the help of the right coaches or consultants to help you make that call will drive 80/20 impact and sustainability.

Get support

I heard Gary Vaynerchuk speak at a conference. Gary is CEO of Vayner-Media and a host of other things he's built. In a room filled with budding business builders and wannabe entrepreneurs, Gary said:

"Chances are you are going to fail. If this is your first business, it's your first time. You haven't trained for this. It's not going to go 'perfectly to plan.' Get help."

The same holds for leading a SHIFT™ and freeing yourself as the Founder. If you're a Founder who has built, run, and trapped yourself in one or more businesses, it's highly likely you don't know *how* to run your businesses without remaining in them day to day.

To take off your training wheels and have no one running next to you holding the bicycle might feel dangerous. If you fall off, it can stop you from wanting to get on the bicycle ever again. To prevent this from happening, it's crucial to get support on the technical fundamentals of the process of letting go, as well as having the emotional support and coaching to let go.

> **"A HEART ATTACK IS A REMINDER THAT LIFE IS SHORT. DON'T WASTE IT DOING ANYTHING OTHER THAN WHAT SETS YOUR SOUL ON FIRE."—UNKNOWN**

Don't wait for a heart attack to be your "support."

Identify your next big thing

Without a goal, attempting to free yourself from your business is no different from giving up smoking (or trying to). Relying on long-term ideals is generally a terrible forcing mechanism for short-term behavior changes. We know this.

As the saying goes, idle hands do the devil's work. If you're a Founder leaving your business, you must be *going to* something.

As a Founder, your work is no doubt a massive part of your identity and purpose. Founders are, by definition, driven go-getters. If you don't have something new to "go and get," you will struggle to let go of the status quo and subconsciously undermine the process.

The personal work in the SHIFT™ process is twofold:

Get hit by a proverbial bus

Book an eight-week holiday (typically months ten and eleven of a SHIFT™ implementation), without your laptop. Travel three continents, take golf lessons, write a book—whatever you want—but you cannot be in contact with the business. You have effectively been hit by a bus, and the business needs to continue without you. Like sending your kid off to their first sleepover, school camp, or university, this will be hard, but it's very necessary. Do it.

Then, start a new chapter

Launch a new business. Start a charity. Move to a golf estate. Rent a yacht and sail abroad. Even if you are staying in an advisory board role in the business (which is always advisable), you must have something to keep you busy, stimulated, and purposeful for eight hours a day. This is hard to figure out, but figure it out you must. Again, get some help. Find a sounding board. Free up time during the SHIFT™ to lay foundations and have something new to sink your teeth into after you've been hit by the proverbial bus.

Commit—and "get" accountability

The first set of Founders I freed were extremely lucky to have found me. Why? Because I literally took the business away from them. I excluded them from meetings. I locked the CEO out of the boardroom because he insisted on answering questions that should have been answered by my new managers.

I kicked them out of their business.

Thankfully, for them, once we agreed on a way forward, I have a very ruthless way of implementing change and holding people accountable—especially senior people.

If the board and I had waited for them to "happily hand over the business," they would still be at thirty employees, not hundreds of employees across continents.

You must commit to the SHIFT™ and being freed, and you need to find someone to hold you accountable. Someone with teeth.

Relying on the senior managers in the business to play that role can destroy these key relationships when things get heated. A breakdown in those relationships is highly unhelpful.

A coach can be helpful, but you still need to hold yourself accountable day to day. And many of your (now) default leadership behaviors may undermine the process without you even knowing.

Some Founders set up boards or bring in an independent non-executive to walk the road and utilize their expertise.

The greatest success comes from some form of independent consultant that has insight into the business, a medium- to long-term commitment to the success of the business and the program, *and* some form of decision-making rights.

I can guarantee you that at some point in the process, the following words will come to mind:

"It's my business, and I will do what I want to."

That's **the trap** talking.

In these situations, the Founder (you), the business, and the SHIFT™ need a strong "bad cop" to roll up their sleeves, get into the fray, and fight for the common good of all.

Remember it is possible

There are over 30 million businesses registered in the United States, and each one of those businesses runs without me as its COO. In the same vein, it is possible for your business to run successfully without you, the Founder, at the helm.

This book is dedicated to my dear friend Richard, who worked extremely hard to achieve freedom within his own business. Allow me to share one final story with you:

I skydived for many years—one of my many weird hobbies. Exciting, social, "away from it all," and with an interesting cross-section of society.

I met Richard through skydiving. It was only after a couple of months that we started talking work, and Richard informed me that he was the CEO of a large, family-owned business. Over a few bottles of wine, we swapped war stories of growing businesses and managing people—the usual. Richard revealed his frustrations with people challenges and growth—how much time he was sacrificing to running the business instead of growing the business, and the opportunities outside of the core business he could clearly see.

Richard and I became good friends, and, learning more about his business, I provided personal guidance and consulting.

One Christmas, I received a surprise gift from Richard—a kiridashi, a single-bevel Japanese utility knife. This one was custom-made to be used in fly-tying—I have been an avid fly fisherman for years and tie my own flies. Funnily enough, Richard was not a fly fisherman, so this was a very thoughtful gift indeed. Along with it was a handwritten note, thanking me for my support.

Tom,

So, I'm not the Xmas Gift type, but, I do think a memento for all the years of advise you've given me is in order.

...is fancy stuff. It has a lifetime warranty on the edge, so, when it stops slicing, send it back and he will sharpen it, hows that for service!

Thanks for being around,

Rich

A few years later, Richard died in a helicopter accident.

Flying helicopters was one of his many hobbies. He left behind his family business and his family—a wife and four young children.

Thankfully, Richard had removed himself from the core functions of the business, and had been enjoying life. Time with his family. Skydiving. Travel. Flying helicopters. Burning Man. He built a full-on commercial kitchen to provide for his staff during COVID. All while the business continued to grow and thrive with the systems and structures Richard had the foresight to implement.

His legacy, and his ability to continue to provide for his family and his team, lives on.

It's an emotional and thought-provoking story for all Founders.

YOUR BUSINESS CAN RUN, GROW, AND FLOURISH WITHOUT YOU LEADING IT DAY TO DAY.

YOUR LEGACY, YOUR IMPACT ON THE WORLD AND ON YOUR PEOPLE, INEVITABLY MEANS THAT YOUR BUSINESS NEEDS TO GROW AND FLOURISH WITHOUT YOU.

THERE IS NO BETTER TIME TO START THAT PROCESS THAN RIGHT NOW.

SO, WHAT'S NEXT?

You now have all the pieces and principles to start looking at your business from a SHIFT™ perspective.

EACH UNIQUE FOUNDER, BUSINESS, AND MANAGEMENT TEAM NEEDS TO TAILOR THEIR SHIFT™ APPROACH TO SUIT THEIR BUSINESS AND THEIR ASPIRATIONS.

As I mentioned before, the biggest challenge I've experienced with business leaders who have not worked in a multitude of companies is their limited perspectives of how things can be done. While business principles are always clear—read any business book from Barnes & Noble—how to apply them is where the rubber hits the road.

Effectively applying the SHIFT™ principles will, no doubt, improve your business. This is all best-practice, business-operating-system thinking. Freeing the Founder (yourself) means really getting your business to sing. This takes commitment, investment, and accountability. All very challenging for a trapped Founder to do alone.

And, once SHIFT™ is in place, you also need to *keep* yourself out! There's no point in freeing yourself in year one only to return in year two or three, meddling and undermining the progress and systems.

Founder involvement needs structure and management. Often, the Founder themselves needs structure and management!

The first step is a good diagnostic. Knowing where you stand and what to work on is critical if you have limited resources. If you haven't already, you can assess your "Free the Founder" readiness, for free, here: https://freethefounder.scoreapp.com/

If you're serious about starting the process, the next step is getting help. If you have any questions, or would like to compare notes or dig a little deeper, please get in touch. If you are looking to discuss how we could collaborate on your SHIFT™ journey, please reach out for a discussion. Head over to www.exitwithouttheexit.com

And, lastly, please do review this book on Amazon, and share your personal success stories and learnings! After all, it's all about fulfillment, freedom, and true success.

Free the Founder. And free the business.

ABOUT
THE AUTHOR

T om Gardner is an ex-McKinsey "startup COO" and international-bestselling author.

Tom has always been driven by his ability to simplify complex problems for others—from starting a faculty mentorship program while studying engineering, to finding himself at McKinsey & Company simplifying strategic problems for some of the world's most prestigious companies. Tom was also part of McKinsey's global training faculty and co-led an internal consulting best-practices initiative.

Looking to drive more impact, Tom joined an early-stage startup, taking over operations and scaling the business from thirty to 500-plus staff. The company won Global Best Disaster Recovery in 2014, and the Prince of Wales Award for Business in the Community the following year. Tom then co-founded Carter, a startup simplifying the complex new-car-buying journey. Carter's dealerships quickly became the number-one performers in the country. He then launched Co-Flo, a legal technology solution to simplify legal operations, serving some of the biggest firms in Europe, Africa, and now the US.

On the side, Tom has been a non-executive director, independent advisor, skydiver, and yoga teacher. When he's not working, Tom enjoys fly fishing, yoga, golf, wine appreciation, and spending time with his dogs.

In 2023, Tom started the Management Distillery, a consulting firm with a mission to free the Founders of high-potential, medium-sized businesses.

If you are looking for insight into developing your leadership team, be sure to grab a copy of Tom's international bestseller *From Manager to Executive* at https://www.amazon.com/Manager-Executive-Take-Career-Level/dp/1998756912

www.ingramcontent.com/pod-product-compliance
Lightning Source LLC
Chambersburg PA
CBHW020846210326
41597CB00041B/949